ANGEL & Me

Stories by
Sara Maitland

MOREHOUSE PUBLISHING
HARRISBURG, PA

F
Mai

GLORIA DEI LUTHERAN
CHURCH LIBRARY
DOWNERS GROVE, IL
7605

© Sara Maitland 1995

All rights reserved. No part of this publication may be
reproduced or transmitted in any form or by any means,
electronic or mechanical including photocopying, recording,
or any information storage or retrieval system, without prior
permission in writing from the publishers.

First published in 1996 in the UK by Mowbray,
a Cassell imprint.

First published in the U.S.A. 1997 by
Morehouse Publishing

EDITORIAL OFFICE
871 Ethan Allen Highway
Ridgefield, CT 06877

CORPORATE OFFICE
PO Box 1321
Harrisburg, PA 17105

A catalog record for this book is available from
the Library of Congress.

Printed in the United States of America

CONTENTS

This book is dedicated, with love and thanks, to Stephen Sheedy and Angela Poindestre in whose lovely and orderly house I wrote a number of these stories, who were my sponsors at my reception into the Roman Catholic Church and who have been my friends for over a quarter of a century.

The sources of Christianity are largely without abstractions. We have a collection of stories, sayings, parables, letters and poems arising out of living experience. By sucking out — abstracting — the content Western theologians discard context and form as irrelevant and clothe them with the trappings of philosophical knowledge. All other forms of Christian truth are treated as second class. But the biblical texts are artful. The bible's artfulness is our inspiration.

ANGELA WEST

THE STORY OF THESE STORIES

In 1988 I was asked to write a story for Good Friday to be broadcast on BBC Radio 4. There had been a long custom whereby the old 'Morning Story' slot was given to religious programming during Holy Week. Until 1988 these fifteen minutes had been used for sermons or talks, but the religious programming department decided that since it was a fiction slot they would use it for 'theological' short stories. That first year they produced a miscellany mainly of older material, but commissioned one new story, 'Mary of Magdala', which was read (wonderfully) by Miriam Margolyes.

'Mary of Magdala' was in fact an adaptation of a piece I had written in the 1970s. My first novel *Daughter of Jerusalem* had, at the end of each chapter, very short stories about biblical women — the theme of the book was infertility, the great biblical narrative of barrenness — and a story about Mary Magdalene had been one of these meditative passages. This seems important to me now — these stories began as fiction, not as theology.

The following year the BBC commissioned me to do a series of five stories which was broadcast daily through Holy Week in 1989, and which is published here as 'Women of the Passion'; and in 1991 asked me to do a second sequence — 'Angel and me', which was broadcast under the title 'Conversations with an angel'. I have since written, although these have not been recorded, two more sequences of stories — 'Mother of the promise' and 'Sisters of the Spirit'.

These sets of stories solved a real problem for me: how I could bring together two parts of myself which feel integrated inside me but don't seem to sit comfortably together in public. The part of me that is feminist novelist and the part of me that is a Christian and would-be theologian. Both these parts are convinced that, particularly at this cultural moment of dissension and subjectivity, fiction, imagination and narrative have a vital rôle to play; that they can 'refresh the parts that dialectic cannot reach' and are necessary to a fully human way of living in the material world.

Finding this way of writing has made me very happy. However these series of stories have created a publishing problem: they are too long and too 'religious' to sit comfortably in collections of my other short fictions, and they don't 'look like' theology! Although there are a remarkable number of learned theological treatises on 'narrative theology' and its importance, there do not seem to be many books that actually do it, or rather tell it. This is sad, but should not be surprising. But in this context I am delighted, not just at a purely personal level, that Cassell have found a way of publishing this attempt at 'artful theology'.

For obvious reasons I do not want to theologize on my own stories: I am claiming here that they *are* theology. Nor do I feel a need to defend them as literature, as fiction. However for people less involved in the liturgies and narratives of Holy Week I would like to explain the structure of the sequences in this book.

The physical structure is simple: the 'Morning Story' on BBC Radio 4 has fifteen minutes of air time. The story itself has to be fourteen and a half minutes long, so that the author, the title and the reader can be mentioned: that is the reason why all these stories are almost exactly the same length. I found this a helpful boundary not a restriction. When I came to write the later stories I kept to the length even though I was not obliged to do so.

The narrative structure was also fixed by the commission: the stories were for Holy Week, the week that precedes Easter. In all three series I have followed a chronology for Holy Week that is a synthesis of the events recorded in the synoptic gospels — that is from Matthew, Mark and Luke (John was up to something rather different theologically, and his time-scale does not fully correspond to the other three gospel writers) — and from the traditions of the Western Church. I have used this narrative not as an historical account, but as a dramatic underpinning to my own interpretations. Biblical scholars would treat the events very differently.

All four of the sequences are therefore based on the following events. On Palm Sunday, the Sunday one week before Easter day and, in Jewish culture, the first day of the week, Jesus arrived in Jerusalem. He entered the Holy City, then under Roman occupation, riding on a donkey and welcomed by an enthusiastic crowd, who spread palm branches and garments on the road in his honour.

On the following three days he spent time teaching in the temple, and on one of these, usually treated as the Tuesday, the 'cleansing of the temple', when he overthrew the tables of the money changers, took place. He also spent time in Bethany with his friends Mary, Martha and Lazarus, and talked with the disciples. Over these three days the realization that he imposed a real threat to the religious and political stability of Jerusalem led to a decision to get rid of him. Also during these three days Judas Iscariot's decision to betray Jesus was formed. The Thursday of this week was Passover, and Jesus with his disciples kept this feast in an 'upper room' in Jerusalem. It was at this meal, usually called the Last Supper, that he initiated the Eucharist, which with Baptism was to become the central rite of the early Church. After supper Jesus and his friends went out of the city to the Garden of Gethsemane, where Jesus faced his final temptation and where, to his annoyance, his disciples slept. Here he was arrested, not by the Romans but by the Jewish religious authorities. Judas identified Jesus to them by kissing him.

Jesus' trial, first by the High Priests and subsequently by Pontius Pilate, the Roman consul, went on through the night. Sometime the following morning, to satisfy the demands of the crowd, Jesus was condemned and immediately crucified. Although most of his companions deserted him at this point, his mother, John, Mary Magdalene and some other women watched the whole brutal process of his execution. By Friday evening he was dead and, after piercing his side with a spear to make sure that the death sentence had been fully carried out, he was taken down from the cross and his body was handed back to his friends for burial. He was buried nearby in a pre-dug tomb belonging to a wealthy 'fellow-traveller' called Joseph of Arimathaea. The Romans provided a guard for the tomb, a cave rather than a hole in the ground, which was sealed with a large stone.

Technically Holy Week ends here. According to a brief account in the Apostles' Creed, and to a long tradition more strongly developed in the Orthodox Churches of the East, between the burial and the resurrection Jesus 'descended into hell' and 'harrowed' it: rescuing the souls of the virtuous from a damnation that they had not earned.

At some point during Saturday night or early on Sunday morning, 'while it was still dark', unseen and unexplained, Jesus rose from the dead, leaving the tomb empty except for the grave cloths in which he had been wrapped. In the following hours he appeared first to Mary of Magdala in the garden, then to two disciples on the road to Emmaus, and to Peter. These appearances — and all the subsequent ones until the moment of the Ascension forty days later — all share in a deep mystery; they are both extremely ordinary, physical, actual (Jesus talks, lets people touch him, eats and cooks) and at the same time his close friends fail to recognize him immediately. These appearances seem to me a passionate and beautiful struggle by the earliest Christians to make stories, make narratives that do not explain but do make sense of something beyond telling. I know that I very much want to write stories about the harrowing of hell and particularly about Easter Day itself. I have not yet found a way, a story, to do so, but the painful events of Holy Week are mediated and mitigated for Christians always in the knowledge of the resurrection, and I hope the stories integrate at least the promise of the enormous hope that is waiting just round the corner.

The stories in this collection, as I hope I have made clear, have a long history. I owe more thanks to more people than I can pay here; but I would particularly like to thank all the actresses who read the radio stories; they not only did a wonderful job, they also linked me to the many listeners who encouraged me in what seemed like a very new kind of work for me.

These stories would not have been written at all without Caroline Dunne, who commissioned and produced them for the BBC. She has given me a gift of more value than is easy to be grateful for — but I thank her, for the commissions themselves and even more for the care, fun and inspired professionalism that she brought to the job. They would not be published now but for the support of Judith Longman, my publisher at Cassell, who is not only enthusiastic and correctly bossy, but also understands surprisingly often what I am going on about.

I also owe a special thanks to Robert Evans, an artful theologian if ever there was one, for encouraging me to play; and to David Maitland for being the responsive listener every writer for radio needs.

'Women of the Passion' is dedicated to Ros Hunt, who apart from her constant support for my feminist theological projects also kept copies of the series after I had lost them.

'Mother of the promise' is offered with considerable trepidation as a loving present to Michelene Wandor, who first raised with me the irritation and pain that the Christian appropriation of stories from the Hebrew scriptures causes her and other Jews. I do not apologize for using Sarah in this closely paralleled way, because I cannot give up my imaginative investment in the older narratives of the Bible, but I do thank her because I know that the difficult politics of that exclusion have informed these stories, and have also informed and challenged me.

'Sisters of the Spirit' is dedicated to Jo Garcia, because she has been exactly that for me for a long time; and because the strong differences in our understanding of concepts of 'Church' have challenged me constantly to refine mine and acknowledge hers.

Angel first made her appearance in a story that I was commissioned to write for *Peace Together: A Vision of Christian Pacifism* (James Clarke, 1987) and I would like to thank the editor, Clive Barrett, for his willingness to understand the place that fiction might play in a creative and radical theological perspective. Nonetheless, 'Angel and me' is a gift from me to me.

MOTHER OF THE PROMISE

৶৶৶

A SONG OF ASCENTS

Sarah is old, old and very tired. She dwells now in Hebron, and waits under the oaks of Mamre to find out what will happen next.

Sarah is old, old and very tired. Her mind wanders, sometimes she laughs and sometimes she weeps and those who love her do not know why. Her mind wanders across all her long life and she struggles to make it into a story: the story of her life, the story of Sarah.

It is hard to make sense of it sometimes.

Once long ago, so long ago, she had lived in Ur of the Chaldees; a proud city with a huge pyramid, arranged in tiers. It was a city of kings and priests. It was a city of temples and palaces and pools; a beautiful city rising above the flood plain of the land between the two rivers. A rich city with a great market, and a high tower where the priests watched the stars and ordered their well-trained gods to deliver the rains, and the river risings that made the flood plain fertile. And the gods, grown fat on sacrifices, and obedient, did deliver the rains and the city prospered and the slaves built the ziggurats and the palaces and the gardens and life was very good for the noble households.

Once long ago, so long ago, she had been a beautiful princess. Sarai, the beautiful princess. Smooth, she could remember that, her skin had been as smooth as the silks that the merchant caravans from the east had brought in. Her skin had been smooth; her toenails painted; her hands oiled each morning till they glowed like honey, sweet honey from the honeycomb; her hair had been brushed and braided. And her life had been smooth, as smooth and silky as her body.

Once long ago, so long ago, when she was still beautiful, she had married a mad man. She had set out, light-hearted and simple-minded, still smooth and giggling, she had set out on a journey with a mad man: a wonderful, exciting mad man who dreamed dreams and saw visions; a fierce, dark, laughing mad man who was her husband and her lover; whose laugh was so deep and full and free that he laughed even at God; whose strong laugh pulled the rope of a bell in her and she laughed with him, a golden glorious laugh in perfect harmony with his rich deep laughter.

In Ur of the Chaldees she had been a pampered princess. She had not laughed then because she had not known there was anything to laugh about. She had giggled of course, as princesses do, she had giggled in the women's palace, giggled and tittered and smirked, but she had not laughed. She had smiled of course, as young wives do, smiled and beguiled and flirted. When they had left Ur of the Chaldees and begun the long journey north, the journey to Babylon and then beyond, out, out into the great desert, the sea of sand, the ocean of dryness and heat, she had not laughed. She had smiled — silent, sweet, obedient, diligent. A good wife.

Out in the desert it was different. It was harsh. It was not smooth. She had wept alone in her tent, wept because her hands were not oiled and her hair was not brushed and her toenails were not painted. She had lamented and complained and been frightened. And soon it became clear that she was not a good wife.

She was not a good wife. A good wife has children. Sarah did not have children. Therefore she was not a good wife. Because she was not a good wife, she did not have to be silent, sweet, obedient or diligent and so, once she had stopped complaining and lamenting and being frightened, she could learn to laugh. That was what Abraham taught her.

In Ur of the Chaldees it had been easy to be good. Everything had been easy. But in the desert it was not easy. It was fierce, burning, dangerous, wild. The days were hot and the hanging gardens of the land between the two rivers were far away; the sweet tinkling fountains were far away and their music was drowned in the winds that pressed gritty sand into your hair, your eyes, your ears, your skin, that turned you from a sweet smooth woman into a rough gritty one. The nights were cold and the orderly singing of the priests of the land between the two rivers was far away and their fine chants and clear certainties were drowned in the cold glare of the huge stars and their little gods were lost and they had had to dream out a god big enough for this enormous place.

Sarah learned to laugh. And she learned to love Abraham as only a woman who laughs can love a man. A love that is not sweet or good or obedient, but is courageous and high-handed and demanding and free and sexy.

They were in the desert for a long time, travelling north, and it was a harsh time. Many of the sheep, many of the camels and too many of the people died in the desert and the rest of them had to travel on and leave their kindred's bones unburied on the wide dunes or in the stony wadis where they fell. There were no graves, no homeland, no memorials. But they survived the desert, just. The whole troop and tribe of them limped into Haran exhausted. Although they had set out from Ur meaning to travel until they came to a place where there was no city, they somehow ran out of energy and hope and settled in Haran, half merchants half farmers. They did not say they had settled, but they had. They sold the camels and bought land.

Sarah had left Ur of the Chaldees as a good wife, but she arrived in Haran as a free woman. Moreover since she had no children, there was nothing to hold her. Children teach their mothers to behave like mothers; Sarah had no one to teach her, so she failed to learn. It is the duty of children to tame their mothers; and of mothers to tame the fathers, so that the fathers can tame the gods. Sarah and Abraham and the God they had met in the desert did not get tamed. They laughed.

Sarah and Abraham did stay in Haran for a while. It had been very perilous in the desert and they had only just survived. But while the others settled they only rested. In the night they heard many things; they heard the soft noises that their gritty skin made against the other's, they heard the song of the huge desert stars and they heard the voice of their God.

Go from your country and your kindred and your father's house to the land that I will show you. And I will make of you a great nation, and I will bless you and make your name great, so that you will be a blessing. I will bless those that bless you and those who curse you I will curse; and by you all the families of the earth will bless themselves.

Once they had rested, they became restless. They heard

the voice of God in the night and they laughed uproariously together and packed up all their possessions and set out again. They travelled south now, south and east. They were not in a hurry because they did not know where they were going, but they travelled for the great delight of travelling, in a spirit of adventure. They came, with their sheep straggling out behind them, down the east side of a great lake and crossed the river at its foot, then they turned south again. And all the time they laughed and teased each other and their God laughed with them, but prodded them on.

Southwards they travelled, into a new land, a richer land, the land of the Canaanites, where fat nanny goats pumped milk into the mouths of growing kids, and the flowers blossomed in the fields more gloriously than in the courts and gardens of Ur, which made the bees so contented that they let people take their honey, and still their hives were overflowing with sweetness.

Once, as they travelled through this land, Abraham went wandering. He did this sometimes, searching himself and his heart in the lovely, lonely places of desert and mountain and valley. Sarah rejoiced in his going because she knew his returning would be filled with laughter and delight. She brooded things in her heart by sitting still, by tucking her feet under her and sitting in the shade of an oak or terebinth tree and waiting on their God; but Abraham went walking, went high into the hills or out into the plain and walked all night with God, and came home to her with his laughter deeper and his wiry shoulders relaxed, the muscles behind his neck smooth and waiting to be kissed.

He was away a few nights this time, and she managed the camp in his absence, smiling an inner smile and laughing with the sheep boys, who held her in respect because she had been a princess, because she was beautiful and gritty, because she laughed freely and was worthy of respect. While Abraham was gone they did not travel, but waited until he returned.

Late, late in the night, when the fingernail of the waning moon was high and honey-coloured in the sky, and she was sleeping deeply, she felt rather than heard him return. She stirred at the soft murmur of his travelling clothes falling to the ground, and turned in welcome as his warm gritty body joined hers under the bed covering. Hands, arms, tongues, stomachs came together in welcome and delight; she heard the purr of his tired laugh and her own clarion bell rang in harmonious, matching greeting.

'We must get up very early,' he whispered, and laughed, 'very early, very soon; in fact we will not go to sleep again. I have something to show you.'

'What?' she asked, not wanting to be told, longing to be surprised.

'It will be a surprise,' he said, and she laughed.

And in the morning while it was still dark they rose, sticky and gritty from each other's embrace, and dressed in the tent, excited as children are by the hope of an adventure. Together they went out, and in the darkness they could hear the sheep softly chomping, dozing, warm, prosperous, contented.

The moon had set now, the sky in the west was navy blue, with one blazing bright star hanging heavy on the horizon; the sky in the east was paler, only just paler, and the great constellations were still dancing, swinging through the sky over the land they had left so long ago, and over this new land to which they had come. The stars, the stars alone, were the same; the same in Ur of the Chaldees, and in the desert and in this new rich country they had come to.

The donkeys were waiting patiently. His was tired from the long night's journey so he took his cloak and draped it over the foal, the young ass which had trotted behind its mother and carried no burden. He took Sarah in his arms and lifted her onto its back, gentle and strong.

'Come,' he said, and they went out of the camp.

The sky turned from dark blue to grey; the stars went out. The sky turned from grey to pink; a few birds started singing. The sky was the colour of apricots, apricots ripening, ripening, full deep orange, gold, flame, fire, heart of light.

He led her upwards, over a rocky meadow above the valley and into the hills. The birds were singing. A covey of couched quail sprang up from under the donkey's very feet, startling them. The young donkey was steady though and, led by Abraham, carried Sarah proudly. She began to sing, a quiet, deeply joyful, song for Abraham, for the morning, for the sun that would rise and for the untamed God they had met in the desert and who went before them always, and now hovered, she knew it, waiting in the mountain heights towards which she and Abraham climbed.

> 'To God I lift up my eyes,' she sang,
> 'To you who are enthroned in the heavens.
> Behold as the eyes of a servant
>   look to the hands of his master,
> As the eyes of my maid,
>   to the hands of her mistress,
> So our eyes look to you, our God,
>   until your mercy and love come upon us.'

'Blessed are we,' sang Abraham with her, 'for we come in the power of our God.'

'Hosannah,' they sang together, 'hosannah in the highest.'

They came to a high place. Over towards the river, south and towards the sunrise they could see a mountain, a mountain with a flat crown, well protected, a citadel still awaiting its city, with wide valleys running up to it; and behind them, westward and northward they could see the sweeping green pasture lands, the way the hills sank gently down into valleys, where there were streams and pools of still waters. And as she looked, as she gazed, she had the sure knowledge that it was for this, for this morning, this view, this land, that they had come out from Ur of the Chaldees, that they had left that safety and comfort. For this.

And the sun rose.

God, their God, their untamed God of the desert, their God who was not walled and bound to a place, their God who travels, their God who was God-without-a-name, their God who dwells in the high places, was with them. They did not know the way of God's coming. God was there, El Shaddai, the Almighty. Their God came to them, appeared with them on that prominence, looking towards the mountain where one day there would be a city and looking across the wide lands where one day there would be a people, God appeared to them and was with them and said, absolutely and forever, 'I will give this land to your descendants.'

They laughed. She climbed down from the donkey and there in the shining morning she and Abraham built an altar to God, their God who was with them.

Then they went down, back to the camp, and soon they

packed up and travelled on, south still, south to Bethel, where now in her old age she had returned; south to Beer-Sheba, where Abraham now dwelt; south into the Negeb, where famine found them, south into Egypt where they had grown rich; and whence they had turned north again to war and grief.

But still there was that morning, that joyful procession in the dawn before the sun rose, that wide view, that moment when God appeared with them in the glory of the rising sun and where she and Abraham had laughed. Still there is the citadel waiting for its city and the lands where the shepherds can tend their sheep. Still there is the promise: 'I will give this land to your descendants.'

Sarah is old, old and very tired. Her mind wanders, sometimes she laughs and sometimes she weeps and she does not know which or why. Her mind wanders across all her long life and she struggles to make it into a story: the story of her life, the story of Sarah.

BOY CHILD

Sarah is old, old and very tired. She dwells now in Hebron, and waits under the oaks of Mamre to find out what will happen next.

Sarah is old, old and very tired. Her mind wanders, sometimes she laughs and sometimes she weeps and those who love her do not know why. Her mind wanders across all her long life and she struggles to make it into a story: the story of her life, the story of Sarah.

She had been of course too old; too old to have the child. Not too old just in the sense that she had made other arrangements, although she had. Living with Abraham she learned that although their God was faithful he was not at all straightforward. Things were not always how they seemed to be. Their God's early promise to make her a mother of many nations; to make their descendants as the stars of the heavens and the sand of the desert had seemed clear, but by the time she sent Hagar in to Abraham to get her a child by him she had been willing to accept that in making Hagar her daughter Ishmael could be the first of those descendants. She had worked it out, slowly and carefully in her mind, she had spoken of the matter to Abraham and to their enigmatic God and it had seemed as though this was what he had meant, what he had planned and promised all along. She did not have a problem with that; she, sophisticated, witty, complex herself, liked to know that they were in the hands of a complex, crafty, subtle God, who kept faith but not always as you anticipated it. Although, there was always niggling now in her mind the thought that although God had kept faith, she had lacked it — that she should have trusted to a simpler meaning and simply waited. Too late for that when the men had sat down to eat and told her that she would get pregnant, now after all these years, now after her bloody flow had dried up, now after her breasts had withered. She had laughed in the folds of the tent hanging then, because it was all ridiculous, because the twists and loops of their dealings with God were preposterous, they were funny. Their God made them laugh, unlike other gods.

But it was not just in that sense that she had been too old. In a far more basic sense she had been too old; her body had been too used, too worn, too aged. She had been physically too old.

When Hagar had been pregnant with Ishmael she had bloomed; her cheeks full and soft. Always lovely, she had become radiant. Most of the young women did. Sometimes Sarah knew they were pregnant even before they knew themselves, because with the eyes of experience, she could see the richness flower in their faces. Indeed, half laughing, she had told Abraham the night of the child's begetting that now she would grow lovely again, her wrinkles smoothing out and her skin glowing softly.

'You are lovely to me always, Sarah,' he murmured, and his hand stroked her belly with a tenderness she had not felt for years. So she knew that he too thought she would become lovely again and it would delight him.

But she had not become lovely, she had become sick. She was sick the whole time for the first three months; not just the dawn retching which many of them endured, but right through the day, overcoming her, wearing her down, wearing her out. Far from filling out, from blooming like the springtime, she had become haggard, exhausted, plain and miserable.

She had taken to her tent, some mornings hardly able to find the resources of energy to get up. She was anxious, nervous, demanding and short-tempered. She had scarcely known herself. Who was this woman? she would demand of herself; this woman who languished and grumbled like an old old lady? This was not her. She was the woman who had crossed the desert laughing, who had come out from Ur of the Chaldees as a princess and who had arrived in Haran as a tough nut of a woman, a travelling woman who knew how to survive. She was the woman who had gone down into Egypt pinched with famine and had come back up through the Negeb rich in cattle and silver and gold and servants because her beauty had seduced the Pharaoh and he had given her gifts worthy of a queen.

She came to fear, and even hate, the child who was stealing

her from herself; who was inside her like a thief in the sheep-folds, lurking like a rat in the meal sacks, stealing and fouling and growing fat at her expense. Her ankles swelled, her back ached, her breasts sagged, weighted down with milk for this robber. It was a miserable nine months.

And if her body had been too old for pregnancy, then it was much too old for childbirth. Sarah has attended many births, it is her duty as the head woman in the camp. She had buried a dead baby in the desert six months out of Ur; but it would not have died if she had known then what she has learned since. Now, even in prosperity, she would rise in the night from her tent at the sound of a woman's first moan, and would stay there with her; the woman crouched between Sarah's knees, Sarah's strong arms under her armpits and Sarah's strong singing voice, gentle and firm, close to her ears. The women of the camp want Sarah there when their labour is on them; the fact that she has never done it herself is no barrier. They know she will not lose a child who could be saved, nor a mother who will stay with her on the long journey.

Hagar did not forget: Sarah's hands, strong and commanding under her own arms. Sarah's knees, steady and firm either side of her waist. Sarah's breasts soft and warm against her head and shoulders. Sarah's voice, sweet and determined; breathe push relax push push breathe breathe down the baby, said Sarah's voice, breathe out the baby strong strong and gentle and steady and Ishmael suddenly rushing down on the power of her own muscles and Sarah's sweet strength. Sarah's hands untiring, loving, washing her with a soft cloth after the labour, washing tenderly and happily, all over, hands like cool honey all over her. She knew what she had been given, but she was scared now and she doubted whether she could do it for Sarah. Sarah was too old. Sarah was old and cross and ill and had gone away from them all into herself. Sarah was the one who gave, they were all used to receiving. There is something unnatural about the bloated ugly body. It takes a simple love to help a woman birth a child in the tents.

Because Sarah had always been the wise woman who stayed with the mothers who birth the babies in the camp, there is no one to do that with her. And she did not have an easy labour. Her body was too old.

Towards sunset her waters broke, warm and damp against her thighs, and she knew she was already tired, too tired to do this terrible work. She turned her face away from the entrance, where the golden sun poured its last loving warmth into the tent, turned her face and hid it in the bed coverings, and waited mute, like a lamb before its shearers, dumb with misery and exhaustion.

The darkness came, first blue then indigo then black and the stars prickled the ceiling of the world. The moon rose. The moon crossed the sky and set and the sky paled, from black to grey, cream, gold, blue. There was a long hot day, while the women tentatively wiped the sweat from her brow and chatted in low voices because the pains did not seem to come with the mounting rhythm that they should. There was another long cold night, while the women heaped blankets on her and still she shook with cold.

'Walk,' they said, 'you must walk.' This is what she said to them and she would lift them up, place their arms over her shoulder, and help them to walk, to walk a rhythm into the pain, to encourage the baby downwards, downwards for its great dive into life. But she turned her head away, burying it in the bedclothes and would not make an effort. She was firm with them, with young women who would not do the work of their own labours, but they did not know how to be firm with her. They were in awe of her, they were not used to a Sarah who turned away from any task and would not talk and sing with them.

'Sit up,' they said, 'you must sit up.' This is what she said to them, and she sat behind them and held them with her arms under their arms, and they knew that they were loved. But she would not sit up; she lay and moaned softly, hating herself who was too tired and too old for this business; and hating the child who was stubbornly refusing to be born; and hating them for their complacent weakness.

Towards the end of the third night, when the moon was riding westward, Hagar went to Abraham. All the men were waiting, all the camp was waiting, even the sheep it seemed huddled close in their night-folds were waiting.

'We are going to lose her,' Hagar told him, 'we are going to lose her and the child.'

Abraham started. He looked shaken. It was not a thing he had even thought of.

'She'll be all right,' he said. Their God was not straightforward, but he was not treacherous. He said 'She'll be all right,' gruffly, because he wanted reassurance even if he had to make it up for himself.

'I don't know,' said Hagar, 'I don't think so. She won't travel with us. She says she is too tired.'

'Sarah?' he said, still bemused, unhinged by this news.

'She won't even try,' Hagar said.

Abraham concentrated suddenly. His eyes narrowed, and he looked up at the sinking moon and the enormous fierce stars. Then he smiled. A crooked smile, and one of deep knowing. He knew Sarah, he knew her so well because years ago when they were young they had set out together on a long, long journey and it had brought them to this place.

He put his arm round Hagar, still smiling, and said 'I will come.'

Abraham came to the women's tent; he stood in the entrance way and all the women there were shocked. Men did not come where women were birthing. They would all be defiled. It was not lucky. It was dangerous. To the men and to the women.

But Abraham did not care. He stood in the entrance, one arm hooked casually round the tent pole, and looked at her back. Even in the disturbance his arrival had created she did not turn her head.

'You're a soft woman, Sarah,' he said, 'a pampered, idle bitch; I should have left you in Ur where all the women are soft.' He came into the tent and stood over her. 'You're a thief,' he said angrily, 'I've worked all my life for you and you won't do this one little thing in repayment.' He strode over to the chest where she kept her jewels, the jewels the Pharaoh had given her, her silks and perfumes, her hair combs from Egypt; and he snatched it up and tipped it all out on the floor of the tent; there was a crashing and tinkling, her treasures tumbled to the floor, broken, spread across the tent floor. 'You're a soft woman,' he said again, 'a soft cowardly woman.'

She was furious. She turned in her anger. She sat up. 'How dare you, you bastard?' she shouted at him. 'Get out of here. Get out of my tent. Can't you see there's women's work to be done here.'

He stared at her with disdain. 'There's not much work being

done at all here as far as I can see. Do you think we've got all month to be about this business? We're travelling people, Sarah, we don't have time for this soft rubbish.'

'Get out,' she screamed, tucking her chin down, deepening out her voice, 'get out.'

He stood there mocking; a long wrought gold chain swinging in his hand. 'You can't make me,' he said.

She got to her feet; she rushed at him, her arm swinging for a slap. The pain of her son shifting inside her was convulsive. She screamed once and fell towards him. He caught her under her armpits, strong and solid. He held her, while her body heaved, usefully now. He held her, unmoving, solid, tough, he held her; he held her tight and he did not let her go. Her contractions wrenched her, she was screaming, and he held her. Her contractions shook her with pain and she was biting the side of his neck, fierce as an animal, and he was bleeding and he held her.

Hagar knelt at their feet to deliver the child.

There was a pause; Sarah was panting, panting deep, deep breaths in his arms. She threw back her head seeking for air and looked right into his face.

'Soft,' he said softly, 'you're a soft woman, Sarah.'

She knew she had been tricked, she knew that he had tricked her; she was furious and she laughed. They both laughed. They laughed together, deep full laughter, and on the wave of her anger and laughter Isaac was born.

They called him Isaac. It meant 'God laughed'.

God laughed; God, their God, their untamed God, their God who was God-without-a-name, their travelling God, their faithful, tricky complex God, El Shaddai the Almighty laughed with them. Their God who likes there to be, not despair and corruption, but life and laughter in the tents, in all the holy places, laughed with them.

Hagar lifted up the child and handed him to Abraham, who should not have been there at all and she wrapped her arms round Sarah and laid her down on her bed, and washed her, untiring, loving, washed her with a soft cloth after the labour, washed tenderly and happily, with hands like cool honey.

Sarah is old, old and very tired. Her mind wanders, sometimes she laughs and sometimes she weeps and she does not know which or why. Her mind wanders across all her long life and she struggles to make it into a story: the story of her life, the story of Sarah.

THE KISS

❧❧❧

Sarah is old, old and very tired. She dwells now in Hebron, and waits under the oaks of Mamre to find out what will happen next.

Sarah is old, old and very tired. Her mind wanders, sometimes she laughs and sometimes she weeps and those who love her do not know why. Her mind wanders across all her long life and she struggles to make it into a story: the story of her life, the story of Sarah.

Some days it seems important to her, crucial, necessary that she should know the moment when they had changed. There had to be a moment of changing; a moment so subtle that she had not noticed it at the time, but nonetheless a moment so absolute that they all lived in the shadow of it for ever. There had to have been a moment when everything changed, so that what was unimaginable before became normal and, in some crooked way, straightforward; a moment that made what happened later inevitable. Somewhere, on some day, at some well side, by some oasis, under some fierce moon, they had all changed: and some days it seems important to her that she should remember, mark, hold on to that moment.

Other days it does not matter at all. On other days she sees only, in miniature, in obsessive and complete detail, that place, slightly to the left of Hagar's full upper lip, a patch of smooth skin on which soft hairs, as fine as peach bloom in Babylon, lie golden. Some days, some nights, especially some nights, she could even count the pores on that small patch of skin; the patch of skin which she kissed before she sent her friend out to die in the desert.

Now, so long afterwards, she does not even know why.

She ferrets at the memories, sending her will down into long underground warrens, tunnels of darkness, and at the end of the

GLORIA DEI LUTHERAN
CHURCH LIBRARY
DOWNERS GROVE, IL

7605

tunnels she hears again and again Hagar and Abraham laughing under the night sky. Hagar's laugh was quite different from her own laugh, a low murmur of laughter, deep and sexy.

She finds excuses. Hagar was intolerable; Hagar had regarded her with contempt; had sneered once too often at her childlessness. Hagar was a slave girl, and her lack of respect endangered them all. When she laughed with Abraham under the huge stars everyone in the camp would have known that Abraham left his wife alone in her tent and cavorted with his wife's Egyptian slave girl. She, Sarah, was a princess of the Royal House of Ur, and it was not right that she should be treated so.

Hagar was her friend, her golden child, her companion, her daughter, and out in the desert, as few women know better than Sarah, it is ferocious and bitter. They had trekked up from Ur of the Chaldees and strong men had died, their faces had turned black, there had been foam on their lips and they had been dead before their bodies hit the gritty sand. She had watched while Abraham, looking nervous and ill at ease, had given Hagar bread and a water skin. She had watched while Abraham placed the child on Hagar's shoulder. She had watched while Hagar had stood there, not begging, not weeping, had stood there, with her boy child on her shoulder and the water skin in her hand, and had with dignity thanked Abraham for the gift.

Even if it was true, even if it was true, and now, so many years later, Sarah does not even know if it was true, but even if it were true that Hagar had behaved badly, had been bold and brassy and held her mistress in contempt, even if it were true, there was something truer: no woman, no woman ever, whatever she has done, should be given bread and a skin of water and sent out into the desert with her small child. No woman. Bread, water, and a kiss.

There were no excuses.

She finds excuses. Abraham was unfaithful to her and she had deserved better. Unfaithful to her not in sleeping with Hagar but in laughing with her, laughing with that deep crazy laugh, that joyful resounding laugh, out under the moon where the whole camp would hear him. He was in charge. He had banished Hagar. Abraham not Sarah. They were all his; they all belonged to him and he had chosen to do it. He did not necessarily do what she told him; she had never been that sort of wife, that kind of hectoring woman. Abraham was a strong man, not enslaved to his wife's commands. He had done it; she had not made him do it; he had put the child, his child, into Hagar's arms and had given her the bread and the wine skin and sent her into the desert. He did it. It was not Sarah's fault.

She had been too proud of herself. She had not commanded Abraham, she had never needed to. She had managed him. Not at first; at first she had been a good wife, a sweet obedient and proper wife, but she had learned. She had learned to laugh and to love and with that learning she had learned her own power. She had used her beauty and her wit and her intelligence to her own ends, and had been proud of doing so. She had nourished his obsessions, indulged his weaknesses and pandered to his sense of his own dignity. He had been a lovely crazy man and she had followed him out of Ur and up to Haran, and down from Haran through the land of Canaanites into the Negeb and down to Egypt and back again because he was a lovely crazy man; and all that time she had undermined his loveliness and his craziness and had thought it her right to do so.

She had earned him his fortune in Egypt, lolling on the cushioned couches in the Pharaoh's women's palace. Pharaoh had given Abraham gold and silver, sheep, oxen, he-asses, men-servants, maid-servants, she-asses and camels. And for the first time they could not travel light and laughing. For the first time she had thought that perhaps he owed her something.

'Give me a child by Hagar,' she had asked him, 'by Hagar, my slave.' She had wheedled him, laughing. She had managed him. She had thought she could own him, and because she owned him she had thought she could own Hagar, yes and own the child that Hagar gave birth to. She had seen the child gurgle, contented, laughing, on Hagar's breast and should have learned then that you cannot own another woman's child: women do not give birth for you, or for themselves, but for the child, and children cannot be owned. They are gift, gift from God who gives them or does not give them according to a will that is as large as the desert and pure and hard as the stars at night above the desert.

'Cast out this slave woman with her son,' she had asked him. He would not even have thought of it himself.

Even if it was true, even if it was true, and now, so many years later, Sarah does not even know if it was true, but even if it were true that he could have chosen otherwise; even if it were true, there was something truer: no man, no man ever, whatever he owes his wife, whatever she has done for him and however much she has served and delighted him should be asked to make choices between two women whom he loves. No man should be lured by kisses into making cruel choices; and if women will not take their own power and responsibility honestly then they must do without it.

There were no excuses.

She finds excuses. She had done it for Isaac. It was to her and therefore to Isaac that the promise had been given. It was not her fault. If he had been born in due time Ishmael would never have existed. It was not right that the child of the promise, the child for whom his parents had come up out of Ur of the Chaldees across the hot desert, the child for whom his mother had prostituted herself, the child for whom they had waited and longed and prayed . . . . It was not right that her son should have to share his inheritance with the son of a slave girl, just because his father in one of his more bizarrely deranged fits had decided that the mark of the promise was not her womb, but the foreskins of the men of the tribe. She had to defend her son. It was right to defend her son. Had Abraham truly forgotten that in the land between the two rivers and from the beginning of all time it was the Mother, the Great Mother, the Goddess herself, who gave life, who passed it through the mothers, and the men should be grateful if they were allowed so near as to know they were fathers? How dare Abraham claim this sacred thing for men; how dare he claim that the foreskins of men rather than the deep blood and labour of women could mark the promise of God. Abraham would have given Ishmael a share of the inheritance of her son, the son of the royal house of Ur, because Abraham had hacked off the poor child's foreskin. She had to get rid, not of Hagar who was her friend, but of the boy who would steal his birthright from her own son; of the child who would not even have existed but for her.

When Hagar was in labour with Ishmael, Sarah had leaned against the tent post in the middle of the tent and held Hagar by her armpits for seven hours, and their sweat had mixed together. At the worst point, the point which Sarah now knew came to every woman in labour, when Hagar had wanted to give up and lie down and cover her face and die, she had shouted at Sarah to leave her be, and Sarah had laughed and sung and told Hagar that they would labour together for this child and for all the children born to the encampment, for they had not come out of the desert, up from Egypt for themselves alone, but so that they could become a people, a nation as numerous as the sands of the desert and the stars of the desert sky. And encouraged Hagar had gone back to her heavy work and in the first light as the moon set and the silver grey dew was touched to brightness Ishmael had been born and they had all rejoiced; all the women, herself among them, had rejoiced because after a long night of watching and waiting a son had been born to them, a son with dark eyes and a heavy scowl who now, sleepily after his long journey, nuzzled and slept on his mother's breast. All the women of the encampment had shared the victory, the new life, the sacred gift from the Great Mother.

Even if it was true, even if it was true, and now, so many years later, Sarah does not even know if it was true, but even if it were true that a woman must defend her own children, must favour them over the children of other women, must struggle and suffer especially for them; even if it were true, there was something truer: all women are sisters because they are all daughters of the Great Mother, and no woman in defence of her own child may kiss another woman on the cheek, just to the left of her mouth, and smile and send her and her child out into the desert to die.

There were no excuses.

She excuses herself. After all, in the end, it did not matter. Nowadays she hears that Ishmael swaggers into the encampment down in Beer-Sheba, a lordly man, fierce and frowning against the midday sun, a desert ranger, his hand against all men; a chieftain in Paran with his lovely Egyptian wife and his trail of children. So she did not kill him, nor Hagar and it did not really matter. He comes and goes, still Abraham's son; he and Isaac, content, easy with each other, cuffing each other's shoulders. He does not come up to Hebron to visit her, but she would not wish him to. She has heard that Hagar has been laid to rest now, after a long and honourable life, and she saw her son married and dandled her grandchildren and was content. So it did not really matter.

It mattered.

It mattered because betrayal always matters. She had kissed Hagar tenderly and smiled.

It mattered. God, their God, their untamed God, their God who was not walled and bound to a place, their God who travels, their God who is God-without-a-name, their God who dwells in the high places, El Shaddai, the Almighty went out with Hagar into the desert. They should have known their God would do so. They had stopped laughing. They had become too rich; they had stopped travelling; they had laid claim to a land, a land flowing with milk and honey. They had formed a war-band; they had made treaties, alliances and blood-strewn sacrifices to their own advantage with people who had tame gods. They bargained with El Shaddai the Almighty, offering the God-without-a-name petty bargains — a foreskin for your name O God; a dead child on a wind-swept sand-dune, a tiny pile of bones bleached on miles of gritty sand for a true inheritance, O Lord.

In her dreams sometimes Sarah saw Hagar in the desert. She saw the woman she had known and loved, the woman whose armpits were engraved in the pains of Sarah's now ancient wrists, the woman whom she had kissed when she sent her to her death for no excuses that were good enough because there are no such excuses. Sarah saw her in the desert walking with their God. She saw the God who had appeared to her and Abraham at Bethel and laughed with them, walking now with Hagar, walking slowly so the shadow of the Almighty fell over her and protected her from the fierceness of the midday sun. She saw God opening the sand to find water for Hagar and comforting her and promising her that she should be the mother of many nations.

She knew that God did not do this to punish her, nor Abraham, but simply because that was how God was. God would walk with the traveller in the desert; God would talk with the lonely and the betrayed; God would appear to the deserted, and would comfort those who mourned.

On her best days she believes that their God is big enough to cope even with this treachery, this spoiling of a huge and beautiful thing. Some other days she cannot bring herself to believe this and thinks that sometime, somewhere, another little people will have to set off from another great city and burn in the desert as they burned and dance in a new country where there is a hill without a city as they had danced; and learn all over again that God is not to be tamed but to be laughed with.

On both these sorts of days she also knows that whichever of these is true, or if there is something else she does not know of, whatever turns out to be the truth, there is something truer: she should not have done it. She should not have driven Hagar out into the desert with a kiss.

When she had kissed Hagar, when the whole community of the camp had watched her kiss Hagar and send her out into the burning hell of the desert with her small child on her shoulder, it was not just Hagar she betrayed. It was the promise. It was God. It was herself.

Sarah is old, old and very tired. Her mind wanders, sometimes she laughs and sometimes she weeps and she does not know which or why. Her mind wanders across all her long life and she struggles to make it into a story: the story of her life, the story of Sarah.

COOK BOOK

Ⴚ৯Ⴚ

Sarah is old, old and very tired. She dwells now in Hebron, and waits under the oaks of Mamre to find out what will happen next.

Sarah is old, old and very tired. Her mind wanders, sometimes she laughs and sometimes she weeps and those who love her do not know why. Her mind wanders across all her long life and she struggles to make it into a story: the story of her life, the story of Sarah.

Sarah's household, who love her — although not without a touch of that fear which the very old age of a beloved and respected woman makes sweet — bring her bread soaked in milk and sweetened with honey. They worry that she does not eat enough; she mumbles the soft mush in her toothless mouth and occasionally the sweet milk dribbles down her chin. It is hard for her household not to find this pathetic and to add pity to the love and fear they already feel. But when she wipes her chin and hands back the bowl with her long hand, honey-coloured but sprinkled now with dark patches like the sheep themselves, and sits straight in the shade of the ancient oaks, then they remember that she is, as she always was, a beautiful woman, and a hard gritty woman who has travelled all her life and that pity is not an appropriate emotion.

Sometimes when Sarah mumbles and drools on the slops they bring her she is resentful of her own body. Sometimes when she tastes the honey in the milk she is filled with joy and knows that there is nothing better in old age than to be brought sweetness in a bowl, and to sit looking down the long pathway, to watch and learn if her son will come up from Beer-Sheba today to visit her.

Sometimes Sarah sits and dreams of the past and of all the meals she has eaten and all the meals she has made. She has learned many things in her long life, and most of them are useless now, but they do not leave her, and indeed form way-markers for the last journey she is making, the journey across the wild terrain of her own life which has brought her for a second time to sit under the oaks of Mamre.

In Ur of the Chaldees she had learned the intricacies of banquets; the long and complicated rituals that must accompany the feeding of princes. In Ur she was a princess and this knowledge was not of much practical value, because there was always a eunuch, a slave, a master cook who knew the rules better than any mere princess could and would have much resented any instruction or elucidation from her. But in the desert all these refinements had become useful, and Sarah had learned to serve four wrinkled beans stewed in brackish water as though it were a banquet, for the elaborate rituals filled the heart, and the empty stomach forgot that it cried out in pain for meat, for bread, for honey and oil.

In the desert she had learned that food was precious, was deserving of love and attention. This was not something she could have learned in Ur of the Chaldees where there was always food, plenteous food and choice and abundance and delight. This knowing had come to her, carried on the gritty desert wind, as a new thing, one of the first of the many new things she had learned since they had come out from Ur and begun the long journey northward. In the desert, since they had no food, this knowledge was not of much practical value. But later when she was in charge of the household of a sheep-prince, when they had fatted kid stewed in dates, and salt and palm nuts and wild honey and asses' milk and bitter herbs and fine meal and yeast for the bread, then the knowledge was useful and she learned to serve the hungry passer-by, or the men who came to negotiate wells and pathways and boundaries, in a way that gave honour to the guest without making the neighbour jealous. If you are a homeless household, the children of a God who travels, the children of a God who has promised all the land where you now need to beg for a passageway to you and your descendants forever it is important that you treat the neighbours with honour and do not make them jealous.

Sarah has learned that when a baby calls you screaming in the night, then in great simplicity you open the front of your garment and feed it the milk it craves.

Sarah has learned that when a child comes to you with a bruised knee or a bruised spirit, it is better and more useful to open your lap and place the child on that throne and offer it a small honey-cake to be eaten there, before you speak to it of its noble inheritance, of its glorious future and the consequent need to pretend at least to a stern courage.

Sarah has learned that when a man goes out to the sheep pastures, to the hunting grounds, or on a long journey it is better to give him flat unleavened bread and dried dates, wrapped closely in a cloth, and a water jar whose sides are thick, than to give him soft bread and delicate meats and wine. And she has learned too that when a man comes in dusty and weary after weeks of sheep watching, of hunting, of journeying, his bones so tired from the walking that he can hardly sit, and leans against the tent pole and shakes the dust from his hair as a wet dog shakes water, he will sell his birthright for a mess of pottage, for a simple bowl of thick soup served hot and steaming, straight from the fire.

Sarah has learned that when God comes to eat with the people you serve him simple food and you serve it swiftly and calmly, for this is the God who travels, El Shaddai, the Almighty, and he is moving on. He wants to be given what he gave. Other gods were gods of places; they stayed put and temples were appropriate, but this God had been with them out in the desert and knew that the wind will destroy all temples and that there is no time for elaborated rituals. Their God knows that there is a better use for fat oxen in a hungry tribe than to sacrifice them and burn the fat on altars. Their God wants the people nourished so that they are fit for travelling. Their God wants them to travel light, so that they can travel far. Their God comes to eat with them, to eat the fruits of the earth and the work of human hands. Their God has no use for holocaust or victim; life is too precious, too hung in the balance.

She did not learn this in Ur, and she did not learn it in the desert; she did not learn it from Abraham, nor from her own wisdom. She learned it in Canaan, in the land of the Amorites, in the land that would one day be theirs. She learned it from Melchizedek, the priest-king of Salem, who brought bread and wine and blessing to the victory feast in the Valley of Shaveh.

It had been the first time that Abraham had led out his young men as a war-band. It had been a change, a big change for them all; a change from which perhaps there was no going back. They had become too rich in Egypt; you can travel light with a donkey and a few sheep, you cannot travel light if you are very rich in cattle and camels and servants and she-asses and silver and gold. Travelling north again through the Negeb, through the stone desert, had been very different from their going. When they returned to Bethel, to the place where she and Abraham had built their first altar laughing in the early dawn, they had come as different people. They had come home. They were no longer the people who travelled under the prodding of the God who travelled with them. They no longer travelled light, but with so much weight that the country could not support them as a single troop and Lot and Abraham had divided the pasture lands between them as though they were theirs to divide.

After that, war was inevitable. Until then they had not believed in fighting; pressed too hard they would pack up in the night and move on. They would negotiate or scheme for pasturage and encampments; they would come as beggars, but stay only as guests and where they were not welcome they would shake the dust from their sandals and take to the highways again. But once Abraham and Lot had divided the land between the two of them, had set up boundaries in order to keep their property safe, they had become settlers, and settlers must defend what is theirs and to defend it they must be willing to go to war.

It had not seemed like that then. It had seemed straightforward, a simple response of love to Lot's need. They had been simply angry. Nobody, except perhaps Abraham himself, could tell his nephew what to do. An insult to Lot was an insult to them all, and if a raiding party of the rag, tag and bobtail of the countryside thought they could take Lot and his household into slavery then they had to be shown that they were very much mistaken.

She had felt it too. She did not ascribe blame to anyone except herself. But when they had ridden out of the camp, Abraham and his three hundred and eighteen trained men, and the women were left to wait and wonder, then she had been seized with fear. Not fear that he would not return; in those days she had still thought their God straightforward in his dealings and Abraham would not die because he did not yet have a child to inherit the promise. Her fear was different, it was that everything was utterly changed and they would never laugh together with El Shaddai in the dawn. But the change must have happened before, because there were three hundred and eighteen trained men in the camp. Where had it all come from? How had a household become a tribe? How had a travelling people fixed an altar in Bethel and boundaries with their neighbours? How had a gritty woman and her laughing crazy man come to a place where they could risk the lives of three hundred young men, risk the smiles of the three hundred young women who must wait their men's return?

It had been all right. Abraham, and most of his young men, had returned in triumph. They had returned with allies and with spoil and, most importantly of course, with Lot and all his household. And the allies met in the Valley of Shaveh, the King's Valley, for a celebration.

Slaves built altars for warriors to celebrate, as slaves had built the ziggurats of Ur. Cattle were led in and dancing girls, dancing girls who were not free to dance and laugh in the golden dawn, but danced to the command of their owners. And she and Abraham had been excited by it all. They had told themselves that the young men had earned this parade, this triumph, this feasting, but both of them had thought that it was they who had earned it. It was their right because Abraham and his young men had routed the enemy and pursued them north beyond Damascus and had proven that they, the landless people, had become a tribe to reckon with. They had been full of themselves.

And then Melchizedek, king of Salem and priest of God Most High, brought bread and wine and blessing to the feast. He was not a man who laughed like she and Abraham laughed; he was a man whose eyes were clear even while he wept for the young men who had not returned. He was a man who was silent while others babbled and who sang while others shouted. There was a great silence when he blessed them, when he turned the cattle loose and told the dancing girls they could put their clothes back on. He offered bread and wine on the altars they had made, and God Most High accepted the offering with gladness.

'Come,' he had said gently, when, on her knees after the custom of Ur, she had offered him the cup. 'Come,' he said, 'drink with me. The God who travels knows that women must drink too, when they are travelling in the desert.' And when she had sipped, he turned the cup carefully so that he drank too from the same part of the lip as she had drunk. They drank, she laughed, he smiled and there was nothing sexual in his smile.

She had been ashamed. In the tent that night she told Abraham of her shame and he had looked surprised. But in the morning he went out to the people and gave a tithe of all that he had, of the cattle, and the sheep and the she-asses and the silver and the gold, he gave one tenth of it all to Melchizedek and asked for his blessing. He would accept no part of the spoils, 'not a thread nor a sandal thong', he told them, only the price of the food his young men had eaten and that was for their honour not his.

Thus Sarah learned that when God comes to eat with the people you serve him simple food and you serve it swiftly and calmly. You take three measures of the fine meal and knead it and make cakes; if you have one, you take a goodly calf and kill and prepare it; and if you do not have one, it does not matter. Bread and wine, the simplest things, bread and wine blessed and taken. You serve it with dignity and simplicity; and if you laugh because God promises you a joy so improbable and preposterous that you ought not to believe you are so blessed, then out of good manners you smother your laugh in the tent hangings and deny that you laughed, but you know that God knows better.

El Shaddai, the Almighty, God Most High loves laughter and bread and wine and blessing; longs to eat with the people the simple things of the earth.

Sarah's household, who love her, bring her bread soaked in milk and sweetened with honey. She mumbles the soft mush in her toothless mouth and occasionally the sweet milk dribbles down her chin. When she wipes her chin and hands back the bowl and sits up straight they remember that she is, as she always was, a beautiful woman, and a hard gritty woman who has travelled all her life.

Sarah is old, old and very tired. Her mind wanders, sometimes she laughs and sometimes she weeps and she does not know which or why. Her mind wanders across all her long life and she struggles to make it into a story: the story of her life, the story of Sarah.

SACRIFICE

&⁂&

Sarah is old, old and very tired. She dwells now in Hebron, and waits under the oaks of Mamre to find out what will happen next.

Sarah is old, old and very tired. Her mind wanders, sometimes she laughs and sometimes she weeps and those who love her do not know why. Her mind wanders across all her long life and she struggles to make it into a story: the story of her life, the story of Sarah.

It is hard to make sense of it sometimes. There are gaps, gaps in the story that make it impossible to understand. She does not know what happened between Abraham and Isaac in the land of Moriah. She does not speak to Abraham anymore, and she knows that Isaac will never tell her. Now he is grown he will toss his head and speak of women with contempt. He will take him a wife from a distant people, a woman he has never met and into whose eyes he has not looked deep, to see if they share a laughter which will sustain them even in the desert.

Abraham came back from the land of Moriah smug, contented, smooth and sleek. Isaac came back from the land of Moriah like a wild animal, bound but not tamed. For months afterwards he would wake in the night screaming and his mother, in the women's tent, would hear her boy child sobbing and could not go to him, comfort him, hold him. There was a look in his eyes still, evasive, distant, the look of a man who uses pride to cover betrayal.

She does not know what happened. Once, Abraham rose early in the morning, saddled his ass and took two of his young men with him and his son Isaac and went out of the encampment. And seven days later, at the setting of the sun he came back into the encampment and he looked sleek and contented, he looked smug, satisfied. And Isaac looked glazed with fear and would not let his father touch him. That is all she knows.

It is not all she knows. When she lets herself know it, although in her mind she dodges, crafty around her memories. She knows that that morning Abraham would not look at her; Abraham, who always spoke with her before he went wandering. Abraham, whose gaze, even then, even though they had grown old and had betrayed each other and themselves too often, even then he had a wide open gaze for her, a gaze of respect and sharing, but that morning he would not look at her, he would not speak to her, he did not tell her where he was going. And she had not asked him.

'Where are you going?' she asked Isaac when he came for his mother's travelling blessing.

'With the men,' he said and there was pride in his eyes; the pride of an eight-year-old boy who is counted that morning with the men and will be going where women do not go. He laughed. He had been a laughing child before that journey into Moriah. He had been named for God's laughter, the laughter she had shared, stifling her face in the tent curtains: Isaac — God's laughter. So she laughed with him in the golden dawn and let him go out with his father, like the good wife she had stopped being all those years ago in the hot desert north of Ur.

She had sent him off with a laugh; and after that he did not laugh, she did not laugh and God, the untamed God, the God who had travelled with them, did not laugh with them any more. It was not her fault, she repeated dully in the long empty nights afterwards, it was not her fault. She had not known.

But she had watched Abraham cut the wood for a burnt offering, and load it on the ass. She had watched him take down the sacrificial knife from its peg on the tent pole and slide it into his belt.

He had cut the wood for a burnt offering and he had loaded it on the ass. He had not taken a kid-goat, a sheep, an ox, not even a cockerel or a dove, but he had loaded wood for a burnt offering and taken his son by the hand. The child was wriggling with excitement, eager, laughing loudly in the dawn camp because he is going with the men, about men's business, and even his mother who knows everything has had to ask him where he is going. He is innocent, bright-eyed, playful and trusting. He waves to her, trembling with joy, as the small party reach the turn of the river and disappear. And she had pretended to notice nothing because she could not bear the look of disdain her husband would turn on her if she questioned him. She had preferred ignorance and denial and thus she had consented, colluded, participated.

Seven days. She knows she will never see her son again. She will never see Hagar again. She will never see Ishmael again. She will never see her family in Ur of the Chaldees, nor Lot's wife who is turned to rock and crumbles on the sharp cliff above Sodom. The laughter of a God is treacherous laughter.

Then burning in her is the knowledge that God, their God, their untamed God of the desert, their God who was not walled and bound to a place, their God who travels, their God who was God-without-a-name, their God who dwells in the high places, El Shaddai, the Almighty, the God who laughs with the people, does not order the death of children, does not deceive and hoodwink small boys in joy and excitement. Their God, who had grave doubts about sacrifice, about holocaust and victim, who is contented to eat bread and wine, and tease her, in the shade of a terebinth tree; that God, the God who had travelled with them in the desert, would never act so. And if this truth is true, and she knows that it is, then Abraham is not only wrong, he is monstrous. He has remade God in his own mad image, and she had failed to notice. She too had become monstrous, had sent Hagar out into the desert to die and had tried to excuse herself, to justify herself.

What had they both wanted? They had wanted to turn their God into a monster, so that nothing, nothing would be their fault; a God who had appeared to them, had travelled with them, had eaten their food and laughed with them had not been enough. She remembered the awful gods of her childhood, gods greedy for blood, who withheld rain or sent floods only for a high price paid in death and misery. She had realized that they had not left them behind, those gods. They wanted a God as huge and tyrannical as that, a God not of the free but of the slave, for the slaves were not guilty, were not responsible, were not heirs but property. They had tamed their God because they wanted to be tame themselves and could not bear the demands of a God who loved freedom and friendship.

Abraham could believe that God wanted him to take his son,

his only son, and make a sacrifice of him; that God would treat as a son a man who would destroy his own son for future personal gain. She could persuade herself that their laughing God would want Ishmael to die in the open desert. They had been offered a gift and they had not been strong enough to accept it.

Knowing all this she wept. She wept bitterly, forgetting all laughter. Deep inside the tears there was a terrible anger; an anger of grief and loss; an anger of despair. And for the long week she kept Shiva, staying in her tent and mourning for the child she would not see again; for the man who had become so monstrous that he would deceive his own son, leading him out through the golden dawn as though for a game, to slit his throat on a high mountain, who would believe that his God would be pleased by such cruelty. Mourning too for the woman who has become such a good and an obedient wife that she lets her man perform this abomination; who has changed without noticing into a woman who can do such a thing.

She wept. She wept in sorrow and anger. She swore an unbreakable oath that she will never speak to Abraham again. There can be no comfort between them anymore, because he had taken something that was not his. The child was her child and no man, no god, has any right to claim a child's life without telling the mother.

And on the seventh day, in the evening, still weeping, she comes and sits at the door of her tent, so that the westering sun can warm her. The air is golden from the long hot day; the trees around the watering hole cast long blue shadows across the green grass. She can see the ranged tents; hear the warmer rustling of the sheep herd corralled now for the night in the pens behind her. She can sense the silent tension that her strange behaviour has cast over the whole encampment. The camels and captives of many raids and journeys go about their business quietly. The young men and the maidens, work over for the day, are singing around a fire, and women nurse their babies and rock their weaned children towards sleep. The stream that flows down from the waterhole winds across the meadow, and curves round a low hillock and disappears into a valley southwards. It is a lovely scene, a place of comfort and consolation won for them by many years of travelling. It gives her neither comfort nor consolation.

Round the base of the small hill, following the stream back

to its source comes an old man, with a donkey, two young men and a boy. They are travelling light, walking with the long loping stride of people who are well used to travelling on foot in rough country.

Isaac. Isaac. Her heart sings. The camp dogs, who should have barked sooner in warning, start to bark. She stands up, unbelieving, great bubbles of joy, like frothed foam on a waterfall, spray up in her. She stands up. She flings open her arms.

'Isaac,' she calls to her son, 'Isaac.' He is eight years old, sturdy, the colour of dried grass and tough as a goat. He tugs his hand from his father's and runs — he runs towards her and she waits for him, smiling, as young now as any woman in the camp; a mother like any other despite the long and weary years of waiting.

'Isaac,' she calls. 'Come, my laughter.' This is the child conceived in her laughter and in God's. He runs up the stream side, and through the trees, he runs towards her waiting arms. And then, almost within reach he sheers away, stops, panting, and looks at her with wild eyes; eyes that have a terrible knowing in them, eyes that sneer at her. Eyes that sneer from a depth of fear that no child should have to know.

'Shalom. The blessing of El Shaddai be upon you, mother,' he says formally as soon as he can catch breath to speak; and then wild as an untamed foal, he runs, skipping, frolicking through the grass, up onto the top of the hillock, where he turns away from the camp, spreads his arms as wide as she had spread hers, and laughs a harsh laughter that flows over the camp. Distant. Unreachable.

With dignity, but under the shadow of that defiant laughter, Abraham comes up through the camp and stands in front of her.

'What happened,' she asked abruptly, 'what has happened?'

He would not meet her look. His eyes were fixed on a point behind her left shoulder. She saw that he looked contented and smug. He sounds complacent.

'El Shaddai, the Almighty, has given me a great blessing, a great promise, a reward for my great faith.'

She looked at him in silence. It was not enough, he was determined that she should congratulate him, embrace him, admire his courage and resolution.

'Sarah,' he said, 'our God has blessed us.'

'Your God, not mine,' she said, and bowed formally and turned and went into the tent.

And after that she never spoke to him again. She lived at Kiriath-arba, at Hebron and he dwelt in Beer-Sheba. It was not that she could not forgive him, or even that she could not forgive herself. It was that she had nothing to say to a man who believed that God had blessed him for being willing to kill her child.

Sarah is old now, old and very tired. She is not always certain what she invents, what she remembers and what the point of it all was. But she knows with a certainty that does not waver that tears and laughter belong together. She wishes that Isaac would take a wife so that she could have a daughter-in-law. She knows too that he will not do so while she lives. She would, though, like to have a daughter-in-law so that she can warn her, explain to her, tell her. Sometimes she even regrets that she does not have Abraham with her, to help her remember, to help her invent and to remind themselves of their courage, of their failure, and of the untamable, unnameable God they met in the desert, the God who travels, El Shaddai, the Almighty. But it is too late to do anything about that now.

She wants to say: You do not understand and still you laugh. You do not understand and so you laugh. You will be the mother of many nations: will they remember in the grief, and pain, and the dying of their children; will they remember in their own sinning, will they remember to laugh?

She hopes so.

She wants to say: You do not understand and still you weep. You do not understand and so you weep. You will be the mother of many nations: will they remember when they see their children running through the garden by the river in the sunshine, too excited to be touched, alive, renewed, restored to them, will they remember to weep?

She hopes so.

Sarah is old, old and very tired. Her mind wanders, sometimes she laughs and sometimes she weeps and she does not know which or why. Her mind wanders across all her long life and she struggles to make it into a story: the story of her life, the story of Sarah.

WOMEN OF THE PASSION

⅋⅋⅋

MOTHER OF FREEDOM

On the first day of the week they arrived in Jerusalem. A riotous arrival, crazy and joyful.

> 'I was glad when they said unto me
> I will go unto the house of the Lord,
> even the God of my joy and gladness,'

they had sung as they marched up the long road —

> 'and now my feet are standing
> within thy courts, O Jerusalem.'

The crowd, infected with their enthusiasm, began to sing too, the whole swaying procession on its way to the temple.

> 'Blessed is he who comes in the name of the Lord,
> Hosannah in the Highest,
> Hosannah to the son of David.'

On the second day of the week Mother Mary had been tired and had stayed in Bethany with her old friends Martha and Mary. But her son and his gang came back at sundown and immediately she felt the tension. Some of them were high with excitement. Young Simon, the one they called the Zealot because he had once been a fanatical nationalist, his eyes were shining with glee. But Peter was frowning. She wasn't surprised when he led her aside. They walked together towards the fields, and he said 'Mother, can't you stop him?'

'What happened?'

'Happened? We nearly had a riot, that's all. The place is seething with Romans. The Pharisees have never liked him and now he's got the whole temple staff wound up. He, he wrecked the market, and called woe and doom on the temple itself. Whited sepulchres and dens of thieves, the lot.'

'But the priests — they're corrupt, aren't they? Anyway there's nothing I can do. What he does in the temple is his business. He made that clear when he was twelve years old.'

Peter looked at her wearily, angrily, and said 'They don't walk easy roads, do they, the sons of mothers like you?' Then after a pause he said 'Mother, they may kill him.'

'Probably,' she said calmly.

But when he looked down, infuriated, he saw, deep in her bright old eyes, tears too bitter for shedding, and instead of snapping at her, he took her in his arms and they clung to each other, comforting, consoling, supporting each other in the painful task of loving.

On the third day of the week Mary went with them to Jerusalem. Peter had been right, the place was a ferment. There was unease pacing every street, and at every corner there were too many Roman soldiers, nervous and grim. A cavalry officer barged his way down their narrow lane, clanking in his armour and using his whip not on the horse but on the people. Young Simon muttered to her, knowing that she was the one most likely to share his indignation, 'As though we were slaves!' Mary took his hand and hummed a few bars of tune. It was the opening of the song of Miriam the Prophetess, the great ancient song of freedom and victory, which their ancestors had learned when they left Egypt, the land of slavery, and sung ever since in the hope of freedom. Simon recognized the tune at once. He grinned at her, and with his free hand tapped at an imaginary tambourine, and murmured the opening words:

'Sing to the Lord, glorious his triumph;
The horse and his rider he has thrown into the sea.'

Laughing, they hurried as best they could through the crowd and caught up with the others before they reached the temple.

All day Mary sat in the outer courtyard and listened to her son teaching. Sometimes she listened carefully and with pride. Jerusalem was his city. He had come now to his own place. Passover was his season, and he had come now to his proper time. She heard a new resonance in his voice, and in his words were all the cadences of the old songs that she had sung around her courtyard in his childhood: the songs of Hannah and Deborah, the songs of Miriam and the women of Israel.

She liked the style and the stuff of his great condemnations:

'Woe to you scribes and pharisees, hypocrites! For you tithe mint and dill and cummin, but have neglected the weightier part of the law — justice and mercy and faith. Blind guides, straining out gnats and swallowing camels.'

She laughed with the rest of his audience at the image; but she felt the pain of the herb-tax too, and the voice of the temple officers who had ranted at the poor, while damning tax collectors who worked for the Romans. Suddenly the question which had haunted her since before he was born was answered. 'Why me?' she'd wondered, and now in this crowded place she knew — for a lifetime of prayer may make one humble, but it does not make one stupid. She was different from other people. Many women might have been able to teach him the songs of freedom, but not many could have shown him as she had, through them, that hope and courage and truth all went together, and you could not have one without the others. He had needed to learn that, and that was why she had been chosen. 'All generations', she told herself, 'will call me blessed, for God, who is mighty has magnified me.'

Sometimes she listened more vaguely, fitting the rhythms of his voice to the memories of her heart. He did not let the people off lightly either. She could hear the deep sorrow, the yearning in his voice:

'Jerusalem, Jerusalem, killing the prophets and stoning those who are sent to you! How often I would have gathered you as a hen gathers her chicks, and ye would not! Behold your house is forsaken and desolate.'

She felt a shadow of envy. Elizabeth had been well dead and seemly buried before the head of her son had been carried by that wanton around the hall of Herod's palace on a silver dish. She would not be so lucky. She remembered too her first meeting with that strange, harsh, pure young man, her kinsman John. Before he was born she'd gone to visit his mother, her cousin Elizabeth, driven there by a need greater than she could now describe, the need to find a friend who would simply and totally believe her, and her frightening pregnancy. And Elizabeth had taken her in her arms, encouraging, freeing her, and she'd felt the baby in her cousin's stomach, drumming like a butterfly in a tantrum. In the arms of her friend, with this awkward baby beating against her, she had conceived again. This time it was the flowering of her great love song of praise and power and victory.

She came to and found herself looking around the temple again and recalling the song of old Simeon. Right here in the temple, over thirty years ago, when she'd brought her baby to be circumcised, Simeon had told her that her child was to be a light to lighten the Gentiles and to be the glory of God's people. 'Your child', he'd sung, 'is destined for the fall and rising of many in Israel.' He had warned her too, in his song, 'and a sword will pierce your heart, mother'. It was true, but so what? 'Worth it', she thought, watching her son now and remembering the last few happy years on the road when she'd seen her life work bear fruit in his fearless judgements and carefree company. He'd learned what she had tried to teach him. It was the poor, the sick, the weak, the children who mattered, who were the glory and promise. Now he proclaimed God's fierce and biased love for them.

'What a good boy', she thought and was a little cross with herself for her condescension. She drifted off, smiling at the memory, into peaceful contemplation. 'Storing things up', they called it when she turned inwards, brooding. She called it heart-prayer, but they were very young.

Nonetheless she was glad when John came and woke her from her doze in the corner. She was hot and thirsty and tired. He put his arm round her as they walked out of Jerusalem.

'Come, Mother,' he said, 'we're off now. Bit of peace and quiet up on the hill.'

'Don't molly-coddle me,' she said, but leaned more heavily against him, because she knew he needed to take care of her.

She ached for them all. John was tired, she could see. They were all tired and uneasy. Over-excited like children, anxious, uncertain. She would not succumb to it, even though she was tired too. They settled in the dry grass under the olive trees. The breeze obviously reminded too many of them of the north and the hills, which they had roamed together joyfully. The tension with the tiredness was turning to gloom. Peter looking bull-like, and Judas sulky. Thomas's nerves were getting on top of him and Philip's thoughtfulness was changing to fear.

'Mary,' said her son, the only one of them who never called her mother, 'Mary, please sing for us.'

She thought of the sad folk-tunes of their northlands, the songs of a people defeated, conquered, crushed, who still remembered and tried to keep faith; and of the songs of exile which her people had brought back from the long sojourn in Babylon. She looked at their dusty, worried faces and at her own fear of what was coming. She knew what she could do. And although she felt weariness like a weight on her shoulders, she tucked her feet underneath her, straightened her back, and sang her own song:

> 'Tell out, my soul, the greatness of the Lord!
> Unnumbered blessings, give my spirit voice
> Tender to me the promise of his word;
> In God my saviour shall my heart rejoice.
>
> 'Tell out, my soul, the greatness of his might!
> Powers and dominions lay their glory by.
> Proud hearts and stubborn wills are put to flight,
> The hungry fed, the humble lifted high.'

A voice of startling vigour and purity, with a grainy quality in the lower register which had moved strong men to tears. And as she sang, their spirits were lifted, hope flowed in their veins. In their hearts they could again believe that the mighty were cast down, the humble exalted. In their imaginations the hungry were filled, the proud smashed and the slaves freed. The horse and the warrior were cast into the sea, and the women went out with tambourines, singing and dancing. Swords were melted down into ploughshares and spears into pruning hooks. God was glorified, the desert places blossomed like a rose and the children of the covenant saw the land of promise, the gleaming city, the New Jerusalem, coming like a bride to greet her bridegroom.

After she'd sung there was a silence of admiration and love. Later he began to teach again, intense, burning urgency in his voice. She drifted safe and warm between sleep and waking. She loved to hear him and tonight he spoke well. She ought to listen, she knew, because it might be the last time.

There was only one bit that she did not agree with, and that was when he talked of the end of time, and the Son of Man coming on the clouds of heaven with power and great glory, thrones and angels and trumpets and trimmings. But she had seen his coming and there could be no greater glory — she and the shepherd children off the hill who had seen him new-born and sleeping in a manger because there was no room for them in the inn. The word had been made flesh and dwelt among them, full of grace and truth. She had seen his glory, the glory of the only Son from the Father; and of his fullness she had received, grace upon grace.

Relieved that there was still something he had to learn, she fell happily into a true, deep sleep, there on the hillside with her family gathered around her.

MARKET DAY

&ᎦᎵᎦ&

'The cheek of it!' she said very loudly as she bustled through the doorway, 'You wouldn't believe the cheek of it.' He was going to be angry, she knew he was going to be angry. Twenty-four pigeons lost, and not a penny to show for it. It wasn't her fault. She was loud because she was nervous. People thought she was a loud woman, but they didn't know about the nervous bit.

'You wouldn't believe the cheek of it!'

It was a good story though and she wanted to tell it to him.

There was no reply.

The excitement of the day drained away. He wasn't going to understand how it had been. He was going to be angry and it wasn't her fault. She was still puffing a bit from carrying the cages through the crowded streets.

He'd be out in the back with his pigeons, cooing and tweeting to them all right, while she'd been at work. She was tired. Busiest time of the year it was about now. City heaving with travellers, up for Passover. Lots of them needing to sacrifice, so business was booming, the weather not too hot but sunny and bright. Their pigeons were excellent too, he did just fine with them, even if it was all he did.

She crashed the empty cages to the floor and went round the house.

'Joel, Joel.'

There was still no reply, but it didn't matter too much because there he was, muttering away to his birds without a thought for her.

'What a day,' she said, almost pleading with him to turn round, to notice her, to say something, anything. It didn't work.

'You needn't think,' she said, 'you needn't think I sold them all, no such luck, not to-day.' Then still nervous she added, quickly, 'But it wasn't my fault. Just you wait till you hear about it.'

As he turned back towards the birds she went on, 'Not that I did badly. You've never seen such crowds. All the world and his wife was in the temple today. And the price was high. Too high if the truth were told. I mean I know the law says you've got to sacrifice, and it is nice in a way, isn't it? — to celebrate a new baby just a pair of pigeons. Makes you feel special, doesn't it? But I still say it's lucky we hadn't to pay today's prices when our lot were born. I mean it's too much, when you've got to do it. It's good for business even after the money change, but even so, it's a wicked price for a woman to have to pay. Well, if I were a priest I'd fix it up different, quick as a flash. Most women would, wouldn't they, if we were allowed.'

Her husband was unmoved. He closed the bird cages and walked solid and silent round and back into the house. He saw the empty cages on the floor, and almost risked looking inquiring. She forestalled his moment of choice.

'That's what I was trying to tell you. You won't believe it, the cheek of the man. And him just some country bumpkin up from the north, accent you could cut with a knife. And the folk he had with him, you never saw such a gang of beggars; and queer too — one of his women they say used to be on the streets, and tax collectors, crazy types. Some sort of prophet he was. Mind you, he spoke up well. And when he was taking on those toffee-nosed Pharisees, well we did all have a laugh. They were like testing him with all these tricky questions, and he was just laughing at them, winding them right up. You'd have to call him brave I suppose, but that was before . . . oh, I'm getting all mixed around, I'm that tired. Here . . . .'

She untied the money bag from her waist and handed it over to him. He was still looking at the empty cages and didn't count the coins. You had to say that for him, he wasn't mean about money or suspicious, except when he was angry. Even that she didn't mind really. If only he would just talk to her, sometimes.

'I'll come to the cages,' she said, 'if you'll just let me get on with it in my own time. See, I was a bit late this morning getting there, because of all the crowds, but I got my money changed and settled down, not so far in as usual, near the market entrance. And like I was saying, business was good and I was beginning to think I'd sell the lot and be home early. Then suddenly there's this sort of buzz and someone says this prophet fellow and his gang are coming.

'Well, you should have seen them, talk about country mice. All of them just rubbernecking around, like they've never seen anything like it. Mind you they probably haven't, who has? Them towers are pretty impressive to someone from out of town. But although they were pretty quiet you could see the crowd wasn't, and outside there were Romans all over the place. Made me laugh to see them, all lined up through the city and jumpy as cats on a hot roof.

'Well he just stood there looking round. Then some woman came up with her baby. I was just near, and you could see the little one wasn't right — burned or something right down its side, poor little mite. Not two years old I shouldn't reckon, and with these horrible burns all down its face and its poor little arm. Anyway its ma came up to him and said something and he turned round and he just touched the baby. I swear he just touched it, nothing more, and then . . . Joel, I wouldn't have believed it if I hadn't seen it with my own eyes. She had her back to me, the mother, not ten seconds, and then when she turns round she's laughing, and the baby was laughing, and Joel there wasn't a mark on it, not a mark.

'Well you can imagine. The crowd gathered round and I couldn't really see that well anymore, but there were people screeching out about how they was blind and now they could see, and all this stuff, and then there were lots of kiddies and they were singing or something, but you couldn't hear the words in all that din, something about King David, I dunno. Well I was hanging on there by the cages 'cause I was afraid there'd be a bit of a rumpus or something, everyone was that wound up.

'Now what happened next? Oh yes, next down comes a bunch of scribes and priests, all together and not looking too happy about things; and you can't say the crowd was that pleased to see them either, spoil sports, but even so there was a sort of hush, like you'd expect and then this little kid, not ten years old I reckon, who hadn't like caught on that the big bosses had come down — he sung out, bold as brass, "Hosannah to the son of David!" Like a bell it was. Well he was just a little brat, he didn't need a great clout over the head, not to knock him down.

'Then one of the priests says to this prophet, loud and clear so everyone could hear. He says like that this was way out of line, and if he could hear what the kids were saying why didn't he make them stop. And do you know what this chap does? Well, first he bends down, helps the little perisher back on his feet, gives him a nice brush down and then he just gives this big grin, like teasing, and he says oh yes he can hear all right; but he's worried about what's wrong with the priest schools that they don't teach them the old scriptures, like "Out of the mouths of babes and sucklings, you've brought forth praise". I wasn't sure, like, if he was talking about the boy or the babe he'd made better. Anyway we all laughed and the priests looked really cheesed off about it all.

'And then suddenly it was like he lost his temper or something. Someone was passing along with one of those big bowl things, you know the vessels they call them, the ones they use for sacrifices. And he snatches it off him and says something I couldn't quite catch and then he just smashed the thing on the ground. Really loud. Crash, like that. And this gang of the posh temple people are just standing there looking like wallies and not knowing what to say, and then before anyone can stop him, he puts his hand under the end of one of those trestle tables, you know the ones near the entrance that they use to change the ordinary money into the temple money? Well, he just puts his hand under the end of it and flips it up fast: all the coins leapt up, like dancing in the air and come crashing down, all over everywhere. You can see he's got to them that time, and they sort of move towards him, really angry now, and he just holds them with his eye. Magnificent really, he just holds them still and then he shouts out "This is meant to be a house of prayer and you have made it a den of thieves."

'Well you know what they charge for the exchanges; it's daylight robbery, wicked really. You could see the crowd was enjoying itself, but also some people were getting nervous, because the priests were looking really grim. Then one of his friends tried to take his arm, muttering something about this was the temple and all, but he shook their hand off and he said "Temple, pah, I could destroy this temple and build it again in three days."

'And then he turns round and just kicks my stool over, mine, I ask you, and all I'm doing is standing there watching. He just kicks it over calm as you please, and then old Jacob's who was sitting next to me.

' "Well," I says to him, cool as he was, "well, young man, what do you think you're doing? Trying to stop a decent old woman earning an honest living."

'And he just laughs, all cheeky like a kid and says "Old? You? Come on, woman." '

She paused suddenly, looking sideways at Joel but he didn't stir. She pressed on almost desperately. She had come to the bit she didn't think he was going to like, and she wanted him to know that it wasn't her fault.

'I ask you. And then, loud and clear so that everyone could hear, he had the cheek to say to me "and in any case this is not an honest living for a decent woman". And then he smiles, really nicely and he says "I'm truly sorry to put you out like this, but there's something else I have to do." And quick as a flash, before I can even guess what he has in mind, he runs his hand down my cage stacks and pulls all the pins. Honest, Joel, I was that dumbfounded I couldn't do a thing about it, not a thing. He puts his hands on the stack and gives it a hard shake forward so all the birds are tipped and then he turns around and sort of gets swallowed up in the crowd. Well you can tell by the banging and crashing, he's moving through the market carrying on like that. None of the temple people seemed to do anything to stop him.

'The gall of the man.

'Well I couldn't see him no more so I turned back to the birds, but they'd all got out. They were flapping about and adding to all the fuss. It was that crowded, like it always is Passover week, and people were dodging the birds or trying to catch them for me, and the birds were getting into a right state. I chased after them to the entrance. I think they were making for the sun. And then, Joel, they was all sort of bunched together and just when I got to the entrance, and got free of all the crowd, and was just about to grab at them. Well, they just took off, they just took off all together. It wasn't my fault Joel, they just took off. I could see them, all their white wings out wide. Up they were going, up and around. First they were white over the crowd towards the wall of the courtyard, then they came round in a circle, all close, white against the towers. And over the Holy of

Holies white against those great red stones of the inner temple. Then up and up they went, all white and gold against the blue sky. I just stood and watched them. Round they went, fast white against red stones, fast white against the great tower and then all fast white and gold against the sky, like a happy cloud.

'The cheek of that man. What sort of a prophet would do a thing like that?'

Joel stood up and stepped towards her. She was almost scared, but he raised a clumsy hand and put it on her shoulder.

'Nah, old girl,' he said 'don't take it like that.' There was a pause and for once she waited. 'When you told that last bit, them darn birds flying like that, you told it really lovely, I could see them. It's all right, they're better free, flying like that.'

MARTHA'S LIST

&ᘐ&

One lamb — it would have to be the kid, which was a nuisance. She'd hoped to rear that one, she needed a new billy-goat. But there'd be too many of them for a sheep lamb. It would help if he could only tell her how many.

Herbs.

Large roasting dish.

Wrapping cloth. Blast the rules, she was making the great flat pancakes of unleavened bread right here, in her own oven, and they could like it or lump it; but she'd have to wash some cloths to wrap them in.

Washing bowls.

Towels.

Wine.

Blessing Cup.

Hyssop.

When Martha got tired she got cross. To be honest she got cross when she wasn't tired too. But mainly when she was tired. She was tired most of the time, so she was cross most of the time and it wasn't fair.

He was an arrogant, stupid nit-wit.

She heard again his strong clear voice commanding 'Lazarus, come out.' And her sweet brother had obeyed him and had come out of the tomb. She felt guilty, and that made her even crosser. It wasn't fair!

Dishes.

Water vessels.

They hadn't even got the donkey back yet. Come to think of it, where was the donkey? If they'd just turned it loose and forgotten about it, she really would be angry. It was a very valuable donkey and, as it happened, it was her donkey and she was fond of it. It was all very well, but none of them ever *thought*.

She was going to have to go into town at least twice. Today she would have to go down and persuade some poor fool to lend them a room. That wasn't going to be easy anyway — why should some poor woman put her whole household at risk, and there would be a risk . . . a flicker of fear crossed her mind, raising her irritation level yet further . . . just *how* was she meant to say 'Look, dear Elizabeth, or sweetest Miriam, or Hannah, or whoever, please lend me a very large room for a friend of mine and his disreputable gang of friends to eat their, I mean our, Passover meal in. It has to be a secret because either the Roman guard, or the temple staff, or even an over-excited and enthusiastic mob will break up your house if they find out. So just send one of your men-servants out to wander about Jerusalem carrying a jar of water, will you, just until someone sneaks up to him and says "The teacher says, where is my guest room, where I am to eat the passover with my friends?" '

Of course he and his crazy Galilean gang all thought it was great fun. All this secrecy and passwords and mystery. A big adventure: they were like children, naughty schoolboys on holiday in the big city, but they didn't have the least idea. In the first place, who on earth was going to risk offending a decent servant by asking him to do women's work, water-carrying? It was all very well for them, living outside the law and the social conventions, but they wanted to drag innocent and busy people into their games and never realized how trying it all was. It wasn't as though she hadn't got enough to do, without all this.

Then, once she'd found someone stupid enough or affectionate enough to lend her their house, she was going to have to cart all the equipment into town, and she knew that none of them would help. They'd be laughing, and singing, carrying on, high as kites on fancy ideas about the Kingdom, and Freedom, and the Spirit. Even her sister would get all mystical and dreamy and just sit there looking holy and sweet and beautiful.

She tasted the bile of her jealousy and was appalled. That did not improve her temper either.

No one seemed to think that if you had about thirty extra people to stay it made more than thirty times as much work.

She'd asked him only last night 'How many for Passover?'

'Oh Martha, I don't know, the hungry must be fed.' And

then, with that irresistible smile, 'Oh Martha, how much I have longed to eat this Passover with you.'

Who could snarl at such a smile?

'All right,' she'd said, 'I'll get the big barn cleared.'

'Oh no,' he'd said, quite calmly, 'this year we have to do it in Jerusalem.' And seeing her look taken aback, he added 'We have to, Martha, that's the whole point. Get one of your rich friends to lend us a place.'

'Wow,' she had wanted to say, 'you do that feeding of the five thousand bit again then.' But this was the man who had wept when he heard that her brother had died. This was the man who had come quickly down from his important work in the north and, despite the fact that Lazarus had been dead four days (and in that heat his flesh would be stinking), had stood at the door of the grave and called Lazarus out, because he loved her. This was her friend, her dearest friend. She said only 'I can't. It's too dangerous.'

He didn't smile then, he said 'Nothing is too dangerous now, Martha; nothing, except not getting it right.'

She'd given him a big hug, and with her arms round him she realized for the first time that he was as scared and anxious as she was, as they all were. So she'd said 'Well, I'll see what I can do. But you might have told me sooner.'

'Oh,' he said, 'I only just thought of it. But you can manage, can't you?'

'No, I can't,' she said crossly, but he only grinned.

Men! Bloody men!

Oil. She'd forgotten oil.

Oil.

Fruit.

And cooking fuel. She wasn't paying Jerusalem prices for wood and that was definite; and she wasn't begging off her friends either. She'd tell him tonight. Though they probably wouldn't get in till after midnight. Sitting chatting in the olive groves while she worked her fingers to the bone for the ungrateful slobs. They'd get back, dirty and tired and hungry. Noisy, over-excited. Tense. Wanting food and their shoulders rubbed . . . .

Nard.

Rubbing ointment.

Lentils. They must be set to soak too.

Oh, really, she could not do it on her own. Yet it seemed unfair to ask Deborah now; she had already promised the young servant that she could spend Passover with her own family. Tomorrow morning they, Deborah and she, would go round the house solemnly, carefully, cleaning every shelf and corner, checking that there was no leaven, not a crumb of yeasty bread or biscuit, to be found. She would show Deborah the right way, the old, the ritual and the joyful way to do the job and then after it was done she'd promised Deborah that she would be free to go up the hill to her own family. She was such a good girl too, she'd earned her holiday. Martha had not heard a word of complaint from her despite all the extra work. She felt a moment of shame. But no, she would not stop Deborah's holiday while there were at least half a dozen able-bodied women in the house.

And she would not ask her sister to help.

There. There, she had hit the kernel of her anger.

Once she had asked him to tell Mary to help her. Mary had been sitting on the floor at his feet looking soulful, while a dozen hungry travellers had needed supper. He'd said 'Martha, Martha, you're too fretful about things. Only one thing is necessary. Mary has chosen the best share and no one will take it away from her.'

You just run along and organize me a whole Passover dinner and don't moan. Mary is too sweet and holy and pretty to have to work. Be like Mary. Mary is best. Mary is just wonderful. Mary looks so lovely when she's crying that she can't be expected to look after Lazarus. Mary's the youngest, the pretty one. Martha's the oldest, the sensible one. Martha will help Mother look after the babies. Now Mother is dead, Martha will look after Father. Now Father is dead, Martha will look after Mary, Martha will look after poor Lazarus. But she loved Lazarus, Lazarus couldn't help being funny in the head. She didn't mind looking after Lazarus because she loved him. She didn't love Mary much.

How dare he? How dare he tell her one minute not to fret about things, to leave Mary in peace, and the next minute to demand that she gets this dangerous, idiotic and unnecessary dinner party on the road?

I won't, she said to herself, I just won't. Then he'll see.

She even said it aloud, trying it out. 'I won't.' But she had to laugh at herself, a little bitterly, because even as she spoke she was adding to her list.

A sharp knife.

A dish for the blood.

So, she gave up for a short moment and went and kissed Lazarus. She wiped the drool from his chin, delighting briefly in his round, toddler smile, and tried wearily to work out how she would get him to Jerusalem for the party. But she was still angry: the enduring crossness because she was so tired, the old anger with Mary and the newer anger with him, the selfish pious pig.

But that night he got them all home in time for dinner. He and John took Lazarus outside and played with him gently, kindly, till his face was pink with joy. She'd loved him first because he understood about Lazarus and had never offered to 'cure' him of being so perfectly himself. Just helped him to be happy and physically well.

'Martha,' he said after they'd eaten all her delicious food, 'I told a story for you in the temple today. Do you want to hear it?'

'You can come out in the yard and tell me while I do the washing,' she said. 'I haven't got time for stories.'

He left the others and came out with her, just the two of them, alone in the evening light. She knelt over her scrubbing stone and he said 'This is how my story went. I didn't tell it quite like this in town today, but this is the real version. There was this man and he had two daughters. He said to the first "Girl, go and work in the kitchen today." And she said "I won't." But afterwards she thought it over and she went and got on with it. He went off to the other daughter and said the same; and she answered "Of course dear Father", but she didn't. Now, here's the question: which of the two daughters really did the will of their Father?'

She threw back her head, her hands still in the water, and roared with laughter. He knew her too well. 'Oh blast you,' she said. 'Don't you try and butter up to me, old friend.'

He climbed off the hay pile where he was sitting and crossed the few yards till he stood beside her.

'Oh Martha,' he said, 'what would I do without you?' He bent down to give her a kiss, and suddenly she couldn't resist, under the soapy surface she cupped her hands and as his face came tenderly towards hers she scooped out a double handful of water and chucked it, splash, straight into his face.

For a second he was stunned, silenced, his beard and nose both dripping, and then the two of them collapsed into laughter, helplessly hugging each other until the others came out to find out what on earth was going on. And when Mary saw the scene she looked quite shocked.

Much later that night when Martha finally got to bed she found herself thinking of a different list.

I am the way.

I am the truth.

I am come that you may have life, life more abundantly.

Anyone who believes in me shall never die.

Lazarus, come out.

Martha, I am the resurrection and the life. Can you believe this?

But it was not his wisdom she quoted last before she fell asleep, it was her own: 'Oh yes, dear friend, I believe that you are the Christ, the Son of God, he who is coming into the world.'

CLAUDIA PROCULA WRITES
A LETTER

ᴂᴂᴂ

My dear Prisca,

'*Quel ennui!*' you will doubtless exclaim receiving yet another letter from your old friend, but believe me, my dear, your tedium is as nothing compared to mine, so you will just have to endure yours, for the sake of those happy days of our childhood. Little did I think then that I would end up with a tiresome husband in some outpost of the Empire with nothing to do but admire my ever-advancing wrinkles and bore my poor friends with vacuous letters.

Nothing has changed since last I wrote, as you will not be surprised to hear, except that we are presently not in the governor's palace in Caesarea Philippi, but in Jerusalem itself, which is, if anything, even worse — especially as we are here for one of their everlasting religious festivals.

You cannot believe the natives here. You might think that some of them would want to enjoy the fruits of civilization — or at the very least be willing to amuse so influential a lady as myself. But no such luck! They're all intensely solemn and deeply religious, sober, silent and hate us with a deep and joyless sullenness, like sulky boys kept in for the afternoon; and it's worst at festivals like this, when apparently half the native population wants to be in Jerusalem — I can't imagine why, a dirtier, more squalid town would be impossible to imagine, and not even a decent water supply — which is another long story. Do you know our last riot was caused because PP thought that fresh water might be a good idea? He's quite conscientious in his dull little way. Well, of course it was going to have to be paid for. I really thought their temple chappies would be happy to shell out of their monstrously large revenues for a pretty little viaduct; after all, they're the ones that make money out of Jerusalem's version of religious tourism. Not a bit of it; they all got up on their high horses about Romans stealing temple funds and the next thing you know is the whole city is seething with dirty little men chucking paving stones.

Anyway, be that as it may, nine-tenths of the countryside swarms into this cesspit of a town, and then they all sit around the temple discussing their law and ancient liberties. This festival celebrates some antique intervention of their grim and ferocious God, who they claim brought them freedom from slavery, and gave them this country as their own. They chant interminable songs about it and slaughter thousands of sheep and daub their walls with blood. Very nasty. Not surprisingly the tension mounts. They won't even eat with people who work for us; there's a tangible hostility in the air which would be frightening if they weren't also the most appalling cowards. At least the temple chaps are — they don't want any trouble from their own people since last time when it was made quite clear to them that if they could not maintain order, then the whole temple would simply be razed to the ground. Still, they don't like it, or us. Needless to say, in this atmosphere, there's a breeding ground for millennial lunatics, petty insurgents, and what PP would call riotous assemblies. Poor little me can't go out of the palace in safety without an armed cohort, and all of them are needed on patrol so I might as well be a prisoner here rather than the wife of the Roman Governor.

We did entertain their sort of king fellow, a nasty little quisling called Herod, to dinner last night. The most vulgar, creepy undersized worm you can't imagine; quite different from his dead Papa, if all one hears is true. Not that he was exactly all sophistication and amiability and culture, but at least he had some style. They say he actually turned down a direct proposition from La Belle Egyptienne — yes, Cleopatra herself, although I must say, looking at the son, I don't understand it. Anyway the present model is not only despicable, he's weak and further confuses the political situation, which is quite deplorable already.

I'll take the risk that the censors won't open a private letter from a distant relation of our great Emperor to a courtier of our esteemed Empress, and tell you frankly that PP is entirely out of his depth. He wants everyone to like him — I can't imagine why — almost as much as he doesn't want a repeat of the last two débâcles. Though it would hardly seem to matter, if you ask me, since we must by now have said goodbye to his chances of getting the governorship of Syria. Just my bad luck to be married to the Roman Governor who has been responsible for not one but two of the worst riots this end of the Mediterranean in this decade. Poor lamb, one could almost feel for him, except that his general twitchiness and smarminess towards their authorities seriously curtails my life. Strictly *entre nous*, the strains have reduced his virile Romanity rather drastically but because of his sensitivities towards their local customs and manners poor little Claudia has to be unspeakably discreet.

I sound disgusting. I'm not surprised I don't hear from you more often — whingeing self-pity collapsing into bad taste does not make for a lively correspondent does it? But, Prisca, I cannot tell you. It is bad enough to live somewhere where nothing ever happens, but when nothing ever happens in an atmosphere of sullen hatred, it's unbearable. When I think that when we were first married I really believed he would be a maker of history, his name known for all time. You must remember how impressive he was. And now he's earnest, unamusing, and scared in a self-seeking sort of way.

Right at the moment *par exemple*, there's a whole lot of unease because of this young man from the northern half of the province who's arrived in town. He's rather good looking in a hairy sort of way, and can talk the hind legs off a donkey (oh, yes, I went and took a discreet peek, you know me). He doesn't seem to have any beef about Romans, in fact he seems to ignore us all, although Pontius says there's some half-witted centurion in town who insists that this fellow healed some dying servant of his when they were on duty up-country a year ago. But a couple of days ago he and his friends nearly caused a riot in the temple itself, and the priests and scribes obviously don't care for him. Well, now they want us to run him in and have him executed, though quite what for they don't seem to know; which is pretty typical. They could at least have cooked up a decent case and let us off the hook. No one can really pretend that claiming to be the Son of God constitutes a capital offence, and what's more, given our esteemed Emperor, one would hardly like to make such a risky suggestion, would one?

It seems perfectly obvious to me that PP should do one

of two things — either have the chap arrested and strung up just as quick as he can, or tell these priest types to get lost, and take the consequences. But, oh no, he's got all interested and wants to talk to the man himself, which will be fatal — you wait. I mean it is hardly dignified to get involved in a whole lot of chatter about what constitutes blasphemy; it implies that we have some sort of belief in these out-dated local deities. All he needs is a good flogging and being sent home to the countryside. The natives will all disperse at the end of the week, they always do. But PP has got all serious and conscientious about it. To tell the truth, I'm moderately anxious about the whole thing — the people here are so odd, you can never guess how they'll respond to anything. In fact I pulled a minor deception on my poor old spouse: I sent him a message saying that he should wash his hands of the whole business, because I'd been warned against this Nazarene fellow in a dream — all rubbish of course, but he has got so superstitious recently that I hoped it might work. If I just told him what I thought, he wouldn't pay any attention at all.

But all this is boring. I am sorry. It's not fair of me to use up your precious time moaning like this, especially as you and I can both guess exactly how it will end. Sooner or later there'll be another riot and PP and I will end our days in some gruesome provincial villa in exile, and I'll still have no one to amuse me.

Oh Prisca, it is so unfair! I cannot forget how genuinely clever and lovely I was when young: how joyfully ambitious, and with enough of an entrée at court to make things look possible. I didn't just marry an up-and-coming man, I married one I loved. I wanted to be a poet, a patroness of poets and philosophers; I wanted to be a great power behind a cosmopolitan court. I even thought, dear Gods, that it would be *interesting* to come to this strange country where the people are still in touch with an ancient and beautiful mythology, far richer and purer than ours. A real religion. And look at me now! I dupe my husband with nursery tales because he never listens to a word I say. I write vulgar letters full of cheap jokes because I have nothing else to do. I haven't written a decent line in years. I'm starved of reasonable company. I don't even read anymore, except the most trivial trash. Instead I sit alone, and fidget with my nail polish. I know perfectly well that we are stuck here where nothing, nothing ever happens, and we'll be here until I die of boredom or he makes such a major mess of things that we're sent somewhere even more boring. And then life will go on and no one will ever hear of me, or poor old Pontius Pilate again. It does seem a pointless waste of all that practised charm, all that expensive perfume and all that energy that I put into the business of growing up.

You see, old friend, I have a bad case of the blues. So have some pity on me; send me some hot gossip, and even something decent to read. Give my love to anyone who might still want it, and if you have a chance, put in a good word for us at court. Pontius might at least amuse the Emperor with his mystical researches into pagan rituals.

Please, *please*, write soon, with love from your old school chum,

Claudia Procula,
Wife to Pontius Pilate, Supreme Governor of
the Province of Palestine, under the august
authority of our great Emperor, Tiberius Caesar

MARY OF MAGDALA

&⅁&

It takes a surprisingly long time to die from crucifixion. Mary is shaken by how long it takes, and there is nothing to do except watch. It takes longer than passionate grief can last, longer than there are tears or fury or patience. She catches herself wishing that she had begun kneeling, or better still prostrate on the ground, because that would be an easier position to stay in. And now, having begun standing she cannot sit down, because he, raised up there, is unable to move and for her to do so would be a betrayal. He has, she feels, been betrayed enough. Deep inside her own weariness she can feel a knot of anger against the others, the others who are not here, a numb slow rage that will perhaps never go away. She steals a glance at Mary, his mother, and knows at once that she would not have been able to be anywhere else. John has come, but John is so innocent that he probably does not realize the risks, a simple fisher boy whose eyes are still filled and cloudy with the sudden storms of Galilee. For a brief moment she knows both anger and pride — she is the only one who is here knowing what it means and choosing to endure it. And then she is too tired, too drained to bother with these emotions. There is nothing she can do for him except watch.

Later she takes off her veil and pulls the long pins out; her hair, that extraordinary red-gold hair, tumbles down like a wave in the hot sunlight and lies across her shoulders, curling below her waist, announcing to all the world that she is a wanton, a whore. She senses the lewd grins on the soldiers' faces, the *frisson* of shock in the crowd around and she does not care. She does it partly to share his humiliation, but more because she knows that if he can still see, still register what's happening, it will remind him of sweet breezes across corn fields, of the glories of the lilies of the fields and of long evenings of wine, singing and happiness. It is an old joke between them.

The first time she had meant it as a joke. Giggling she had let down her hair, then as now. She had spent the last of her savings from the trade on the alabaster pot and the extravagant ointment. She had bound a scarlet cord under her breasts and crossed between them, so that each breast stood high and separate. She had only meant to tease him, to shake for one moment his impeccable composure. It would be a good joke, they would all laugh together, afterwards. She had waited until the dinner was well underway, until she was sure he would be bored by their prim moralizing and conceited manners.

When she came in he had turned and smiled at her. He had been leaning at the table talking, talking as usual; but he glanced sensing her arrival and, seeing her outfit, grinned hugely, both at her and at the undercurrent of nervousness that flickered round the room, because of course she had known some of the civic dignitaries there, known them too well. Some of them were not only shocked that a sinner, a prostitute, should appear there in their dreary fastness, but terrified also of what she might do or say. And he and she had known their fear and laughed together and they had hated him for it.

And here, here now, on this hot hilltop, she knows that it was her joke, among other things, that had brought him here. That they had pushed their luck too far in the hill towns of Judah, just as they had pushed it in the market and temple courtyard of Jerusalem; they had touched too many people's fears and pride in their own joyful freedom. She, as much as any rabbi or temple lawyer, as much as the Roman Tyrant, as much as the soldiers who now sit careless and bored playing dice under the shadow of their gibbets; she as much as any of them brought him here. And she also knows that he would still have grinned hugely, he would still have turned loyally, he would still have condemned them as the hypocrites they were, even if he had already heard the sound of the nails hammering through the bones in his wrists. So now, although she cannot be certain if he can still hear or see or notice, she has no fears about letting her hair down on the off-chance that he might sense it and be comforted.

She had meant it that first time, as a joke. But when she bent over his dusty, tired feet she had begun to cry. She had lowered her head so that no one would see her, but the tears had eased their way out and fallen onto his feet. She had tried to wipe them away with her hair. He had saved her. He had saved her from her shame, saved her from the disgust she had felt at herself. He had called her a loving woman, because of her profession. She had thought the first time he had said this that he must be naïve beyond belief; it had irritated her, such stupidity. But she had come to realize that it was not that; simply, he knew her better than she knew herself; he knew her to be loving even if whoring was the only way she knew to love and live. Give it up he had said and follow me, just as he would have said it if she had sold something different in the market place. It was who she truly was that mattered to him. Her tears had fallen over his feet. They were not tears of sorrow, but of joy. He had liked her. He had introduced her to his friends and they had become her friends. He had introduced her to his mother. He had not been ashamed to introduce her to his own mother, to ask her to take care of his mother who was frequently confused by the noise, the movement, the late nights and the mixed company. He had asked her, a sinner, to use her rich experience of the world, her knowledge of the ways and timings of people to help his mother. He had not been ashamed that she had been a whore, he had seen the talents she had gained there as things to be appreciated, to be made use of. He found her beautiful, he found her wise, he found her funny. He found her loving. And in his finding she found herself all these things and grew into them.

When the dust had been washed from his feet by her tears, she had opened her pot of ointment, soothing it down between his cracked toes. None of his other friends would have known how to choose an ointment with so rich and delicate a scent. That knowledge was special to her too and she had known that he would like it. She liked him. That was something new for her, to like a man, to have that simple freedom, that not having to be continually wary, not having to watch and wonder, wonder where the snags lay, wonder how soon he might move away from chatter and into demand, wonder when that mixture of disgust and desire would wipe the pleasantness out of his eyes and obliterate her. She liked him, she liked his world, she felt at home there with his mixed bag of friends, some of whom made her look positively respectable. To like him, to be with him, all you had to do was accept that friendship, to accept and be accepted. It was not easy, it was hard. All of them were broken and sad and lost somewhere, all of them defended themselves against each other. But he didn't, he didn't defend himself. With him, for the first time, she no longer had to defend herself. He accepted, and so she could accept, that she had talents and worth outside of her past and inside it.

At last someone at the dinner had protested, protested that he should even let her touch him. She had felt his fingers come down firmly on her head, soothing her against a pain she was immune to. He said 'Her sins are forgiven because she loves much.' It was that simple. He said 'She is a loving woman, so don't be stupid.' He said to her 'Don't listen to them.' He said 'Thank you, thank you for your present, thank you for your sense of humour, thank you for your friendship. Don't worry,' he said, 'don't worry about anything. Everything will be all right.'

And in his pride in her she had been able to leave the room without weeping. She had walked tall across the room, with her hair flowing down her back and her alabaster pot held high. Later, though, she had wept again, in the arms of his mother, who could not share her humour but could share her tears. There was, she had learned, no need to wash away the past. For the past made you who you were. There was no need to apologize for an unloved childhood; for poverty and beatings; for seeking love wherever and however, because all those things made you who you were, made you the person whom he loved.

And remembering all this she turns to his mother beside her on the hill, to offer back the comfort that she was offered, but she sees that John is there already. He is not offering comfort but receiving it, because giving is what Mother Mary needs to do now. It's John's innocence, his happy childhood by the lakeside, his dreamy gentleness, that makes him the right person for this task. What is true for her must be true for all of them, and when he is no longer there to remind them they must still look at each other with his eyes and accept whatever they see.

It is lucky that John is there because she has something else to do. She moves at last, still nearer to the cross, as near as the soldiers will let her. For the next three hours she will stand there, her hair flaming in the sunshine, so that, long after he needs the knowledge, he will know that someone remembers, and still likes him. Just by being there she will tell him her whole truth. She will tell him that she will never pin up her hair again. She will never wear a veil. That she will never be ashamed that she was once a whore. That she was, because of him, proud of her hair which is long enough, beautiful enough to wipe his feet with, and which, this evening, will be long enough, beautiful enough to cover his wounds so that his mother will not have to touch them. That she who has anointed him in his life, will be there to anoint him in his death. That, thanks to him, she is now proud of a past that made her tough enough not to be afraid of this horrible dying, not to be ashamed of him, though he is being hung as a common criminal.

She was a whore and he loved her. There was nothing to be ashamed of. When she recognizes him in the garden, it will be a meeting of friends.

SISTERS OF THE SPIRIT

LADY GODIVA

She woke in the morning, a slim finger of sunlight finding its way through the bed curtains, rooting her out of sleep. She felt wonderful, strong and clean. She had gone to her bed fearful, sure the eyes would find her out in the night, sure she would be fixed by their stare, by the shaking, the rhythmically shaking shoulders, the hands she could not see; sure that the eyes would find her, devour her, shame her. But she woke strong and clean, smiling. Powerful.

He had not thought she would do it. For the first time in her life she had taken a choice, she had chosen the hard thing, and she had done it. In his anger, in his shame, in his humiliation there was admiration. Though she had not done it for that. She had been ignorant, where she thought she had been innocent. She had not known how many layers of meaning there were to a brave act. She had discovered new things in herself; vanity, pride, lust, meanness, anger — so many things and yet, when it was done, it was still a brave act and a loving act.

He had been drinking, drinking with the worst of his friends. Swollen with drink, and food and arrogance.

'Please,' she had said, 'please don't. Don't do it. For the sake of all the angels, don't do it. It is not just. They are your children, your people, you cannot do it.' She had wept. She had been perfectly sincere.

He might have given in if she had timed it better. But in front of his friends . . . apron strings, soft, womanish. She had been stupid. Perhaps she might hope to learn wisdom as well.

'My Lady,' he said, 'it is very easy to be generous with what is not your own. You pay their fines.'

It was cruel. Cruel to shame her in public, to make public what everyone knew anyway. She had come to him from a humble hall, from a hungry household with no sons and too many daughters. He had taken her for her ancient name, and for his own pride.

and for a turning gesture of her childish head when he had seen her in the forest; for the thump of her heavy plait against her long spine, for the turning of her proud little head when she had been barely a woman, still a free maid in the woods, and he had seen her turn her head, a proud and lovely gesture. But he had never told her that. Her pride would break him if he did not raise up a pride to match it and he never told her that he loved her; she must come to him in gratitude for his kindness — his kindness in taking a dowerless girl into his high hall. But she did not come. There was anger in him too.

And her blush of shame, her sudden silence, stirred the anger in him. 'Easy to give what is not your own. Easy charity to the poor when your own belly is fed, Madam; easy nursing of the sick when your own bed is made with herbs by serving-wenches. Easy to beg for pardon on their behalf and walk proud in the town as a saviour, eh. But you give only what is mine. You never give what is yours.'

She locked her chamber door and had her tiring woman sleep on a truckle bed. She kept her pride, and her chastity; and once a month, cold as a nun doing Lenten penance, she paid him his marital duties so that he could not complain. She rose before the sun did and he, turning in a drugged and desolate half-sleep, would see her long back, with the beautiful fat plait, a rope for his neck, her back turned to him as she knelt at the prie-dieu.

'I have nothing but your love, my Lord.'

'You have your honour, your dignity, your goddam mousy modesty. Will you give that for your beloved poor, for the oppressed citizens of Coventry, so that their wicked lord in his castle on the hill won't hurt them?'

Quite suddenly it was serious. It was perfectly serious. All the bad things between them were there, were there on the table, while his bovine drunken friends looked on laughing and the servants held their breaths.

She hesitated because it was serious. She had no idea what he would ask of her. She had to look into her heart and ask herself 'Will I?' Ask urgently, because whatever he said it would not be easy. 'Will I? Oh God, will I?' Then she saw the cold faces of the townspeople, people labouring under the burden of poverty uncomforted by a good lord. The people for whom this fine would be too much — children already undernourished, young girls with wild unkempt hair and eyes too large, old people fearing they would be too much of a burden and wondering how cold the river was, and a long winter setting in. Would he take her in front of all these people? Would he drag her to his room and make her watch while he did unspeakable things with his wanton? Would he . . . her imagination failed.

'Yes, I will,' she said. Softly. The words fell softly in the hall.

He laughed. There was a challenge now. His pride and hers were at stake.

'Easy speaking, my Lady,' and he laughed. 'Words are cheap.' He swilled his cup, tossed off the wine and then not looking at her, not looking at anyone, only at the empty cup in his hand, 'Ride then, ride through the city, through the marketplace, naked. Let them see. Let them see their sweet lady. Naked. For them to gawp at.'

He had chosen well. He saw the dark blush spring on her chest; her eyes dilate with fear. He had never seen her naked himself.

She stood up. 'Tomorrow, my Lord, after lauds is sung.' She pushed back her chair from the table, made a deep courtesy to the company and in silence left the room. They had gone too far, both of them. The hall was silent except for the rustle, the rustle of her silk gown on the flags like dry leaves in autumn. She did not start to moan until she had found the shelter of her own bed, in her own chamber. She could not. She could not.

He had her white mule, saddled, waiting. She came down into the silent courtyard wrapped in a cloak. He stood at the mule's head and waited.

'Madam,' he bowed.

He lifted her into the saddle, and held out his hand for the cloak. For one moment their eyes met. Shame and pride. And silence.

She raised her fingers to her throat, to the clasp of her collar, and her hands were shaking so violently that she could not undo it. He reached up and undid it, so gently it was almost a courtesy, the gesture of a lover. He did not pull it off for her, that she had to do for herself. He had not forced her, he did not make her; it was her choice.

She dropped the cloak into his arm. An evil little wind snapping its way across the courtyard bit into her flesh, and her nipples tightened, pricking up hard and cold. There was goose-flesh on her arms. She sat very straight, but with her eyes down. The blush he had seen last night now covered her whole upper body like a rash. Her legs were mottled, purple from the cold. She bit her lip against the tears and pleadings which sprung up. Charity was not easy.

The gate was already open.

He slapped the mule's rump, and the beast moved forward.

She felt a rush of sensations; the shame, the cold, the shame. And startlingly a most peculiar feeling where her pubic hair twitched slightly against the leather, the creaking saddle against her vagina. The cold, the shame, the strange rhythm of the saddle under her bottom, the shame, the new shame of that rhythm, the shame, the cold.

She tried to school her thoughts. When she rode the donkey to Bethlehem the people would have looked at the Blessed Lady, and thought her a slut and whore and a wanton. She must have been ashamed.

But she could think only of the cold and the shame. And the strange feeling of her thighs, her bottom, her woman's secret parts stirred by the saddle.

As they went down the slope from the castle into the town she had a new thought and it increased her shame. If he wanted her to do this why had he not asked her while she was still young and lovely? Naked was shame; but naked, a blotchy nakedness, without beauty, with her breasts a little saggy and the white skin of her belly soft and scrunched from childbearing was too much shame. She could have borne it, she thought, if they had stared at her with awe; if she could have ridden out in the fullness of her loveliness. But to be naked and pitied. It was too much. And her vanity shamed her too. She tried to think of the people, of their need and her ability to meet it. But she could see only their pity, that their lady was so old and ugly and saggy and scrawny like a plucked chicken — goose-flesh and wrinkled skin, like a chicken ready for the spit.

And because there was all this shame and sounding in her

head, and because her shame kept her head down and her eyes fixed rigidly on her hands, because her head was full of clamour and din, she did not at first notice the quiet. As the mule turned down the high street towards the sheep market she realized for the first time that it was very quiet. It was perfectly quiet. Curious, she raised her head a little. There were no gaping crowds, there were no laughing children, there were no leering jeering men. The street was empty. Every shutter was closed, every door set to. She heard in the quiet the thin wailing of a baby, and the soft shushing of its mother, behind the shutters of a house; and her heart burst with praise. This was their gift to her, their gratitude, the only gratitude that they could give her, and she must know that it was not an easy giving for them either. This was their greeting, this quiet, these closed windows these empty streets, this wasted day while hens laid, and weeds grew and sheep might roam, the people would keep to their houses and not look on her shame. Hosannah, sang her heart, and it was a sweeter song than a crowd cheering and dancing because their fine would be remitted and their children would be fed.

Tears sprang to her eyes, but she must not weep because if anyone saw her, if there were tears in her face when she returned to the castle keep, then they might think she regretted her love. She had no regrets, only gratitude, gratitude and love and friendship. She held her head high although there was no one to see.

That was before she felt the eyes. She felt them, felt their greed and their spite and their power long before she knew what had changed. The blush that had slowly ebbed away came back. Eyes. The mule, baffled but obedient had turned to cross the market square; across the square, towards where the two lanes split, the longest open view in the town, the way she had to travel. She must cross it, inch by inch, at the steady jogged pace of the mule. From a window, right in front of her, the whole distance of the square, right up past the corner to the cathedral, the eyes were watching, were devouring her, were gaining power from her shame, were delighted, piggy, greedy.

Her head was still high with the love she had received through every closed shutter. She looked right into the eyes. And because the eyes held her she could not help but also see the shaking, the rhythmically shaking shoulders; she could not help but know what the hands she could not see were doing.

She had not known anything about shame. Besmirched, filthy, beaten, defeated. She lowered her head. She took one hand from the reins and tried to cover her genitals. Confused, the mule slowed. The rhythm of the shoulders was the same rhythm as the rhythm of the saddle bow against her crotch. She was vile, vile, deserving of this. Foul. Who had she thought she was in her pride; who could love her? not her husband, not the people; only this, only the greedy consuming eyes and the greedy demanding rhythm, that told her a woman's place was to have no place; that to act or to fail to act, to choose or to accept, that under all those things there was only foulness, was only evil, was only wickedness and filth. She . . .

She found a new anger. She would have him flogged; she would tell her husband and he would cut off his ears, brand him, put him in the stocks, burn out the horrible eyes with a red hot poker. Her anger hit a terrible knowledge; she could do no such thing. To punish the eyes which did look would be to repudiate the generosity of every eye which had not looked. They had the right to look and they had generously not used their power. If she had the eyes punished she would deny all of them their right to be generous. And they had so little that to deny their gift, their right to make her a gift, would be a terrible sin. She could not deny their love to satisfy her dignity.

Easy charity, he had sneered. Now she had learned what hard charity was. It was hard. She had to pass within a yard of the eyes; she had to pass with her head high and both her hands on the rein of her mule. She thought of the long winter and food for the poor. She thought of the long winter and food for her friends who did not look. And her ride turned into a procession, a triumph, a tiny moment of honour and glory in a life which had few and had sought none. She rode under the castle gateway, still blushing with shame and with her head held high.

He was standing barely inside the gate and when her mule crossed into the courtyard he came towards her. He had the cloak ready, and almost tenderly he wrapped her in it and lifted her down as though she was precious. She could see his bafflement, his wonder and his pride.

'They did not look,' he said.

'No,' she said.

'They love you,' he said, almost curious.

'Yes,' she said.

There was a pause. Held by him still she recognized abruptly what the rhythm of the mule's creaking saddle meant.

'I . . . ,' he started. He was trying.

'I have been too proud; pride and I called it modesty,' she said. 'We could do better, you and I, my Lord.'

He clapped his hand and the serving-man came out.

'The imposed fine on the people has been paid in full by the generosity of their lady. It is remitted, in total. I have accepted payment of another kind. You may announce it.' He turned to her, 'I may be a mean bastard,' he muttered, 'but I'm an honourable bastard for all that.'

'Thank you,' she said, humbly.

He took her hand and led her, with the formality extended usually to a royal messenger into the hall.

It was not perhaps altogether surprising that she feared she would see the eyes when she slept, but that in fact she woke strong and clean, smiling and powerful.

For each time we honour a woman who prefers her chastity to her life, we should also honour one who rides humbly into the city, stripping herself of dignity, of modesty, of the protection of social convention and even of self-esteem, for the love of the poor and oppressed. For so did he in whose name she rides.

Blessed is she who comes in the name of the Lord. Hosannah in the highest.

RADEGUND

She knew she was dying. She knew it with contentment and peace. Three score years and ten almost precisely measured out and it was time to go. So then. 'Into thy hands,' she murmured, 'into thy hands I commend my spirit.'

'Tonight you will walk with us in paradise,' sing the angels, and if it were not too much effort she would smile.

It was high summer, and they had carried her into the chapel to die. High above her, hazy and shadowed now, the great roof, the ark that had carried her through so many storms, still offered protection. The altar towards which she faced still offered beauty and serenity; the reliquary containing the piece of the True Cross, a gift in her honour sent all the way from Constantinople, for her, shone in glory in its chapel. Around her, her nuns, his sisters, her daughters, prayed with her, so that she did not feel lonely. Out in the guest-house the Frankish Ambassador fumed, needing answers to his now so unimportant questions about the peace treaty, so that she did not feel useless.

Two hundred women, wise and gentle, for whom she had won from foolish and jealous bishops the right to scholarship — enshrined in the rule and blessed by the Bishop of Rome himself, their two hours a day spent not in simpering embroideries but in true study. Two hundred women here in her house in Poitiers.

And he had mocked her barrenness. Silly old fool, she thought now, but quite tolerantly; King Clotaire, son of Clovis, once — and she supposed still — her husband. Ha.

It was high summer. Outside the sun was hot; she could see the sky deep bright blue and the fat white clouds crossing the window. She could hear in the distance the farmers bringing in the grape harvest. This evening the children would squeal and sing as they clambered over the vats and stomped out the rhythms of the pressing dances, and it would be good and sweet, for a little wine was a wholesome thing, and not always the wild dangerous threat that it had been when she was very young.

Tonight at Vespers she will surrender; she will receive the sacrament for the last time, she will bless her sisters, and she will go forth on her long journey. She was ready. She turned her mind to that journey in confidence and serenity.

Then, tugging, distracting, from somewhere deep in the back of her mind, she knew there was something she had not yet done. Something she had promised . . . promised who? . . . promised herself? . . . something she wanted to do before she died. Something she ought to do.

Her mind scarcely paused at the thought of her escritoire, there was a mass of things undone there, but not anything that mattered. She had laboured for peace this last quarter century and she had not been ineffective, but there was no peace and there would be no peace among the noisy royal houses of Europe, so anything that she might not have had time to finish would not matter too much. An envoy, a truce, a boundary decision might not be made, but she was not going to turn her feet from her journey for that.

Something for the convent. Something for her sisters, something important she had to tell them. She could not remember. Her face furrowed with the effort to remember, her still head moved slightly on its pillow, and at once one of the sisters was there, soothing, wiping her lips with the cool dampness of a linen cloth scented sweetly with lavender from the garden. That warm smell distracted her, and although grateful for the attention, she was irritated by the disturbance.

Her irritation reminded her. She had to tell them about anger, about anger and how sometimes it was good and godly and right. It was not true, women had been deceived, they had been taught that in gentleness, in submissiveness there was power, in giving it up, in throwing it away; that love was simply the ability to suffer and to suffer and suffer. Pah.

Radegund was the daughter of Berthaire, King of Thuringia. Not a childhood to encourage sweetness in any woman — that household of savagery, and intrigue and violence. The war-bands did not disperse during the fighting season, even for banquets. They sat down to eat and they stood up to fight; they would fight with the enemy when there was any around and failing that they would fight with each other and plot and scheme and murder and assassinate. For the royal child it had been exciting; standing beside her mother's chair in the high hall and looking out while men and dogs surged about the hall. Her long blond pigtails had bounced with suppressed excitement and she had been woken in the night more than once because the whole household was on the move again — in fear or in aggression depending on the turn of politics and power.

She was twelve the night of the great raid, when the Frankish soldiers descended on the household, their pine torches smoking and glowing, catching the light of horned helmet, round shield, short sword and bright eyes. If she had stayed in the women's quarters where she belonged she might have been safe; as it was they snatched her in her night shift from the courtyard, galloping, thundering, and then out into the night. She had not been frightened, thrilled rather, just a child.

They carried her off to the Frankish Court, to the household of Clovis where she grew up. Her status was strange — she was not slave or prisoner; she was treated with honour; she was held for high ransom at first, which was never paid, and to this day she did not know exactly why. Later she was contracted in marriage to Clotaire, heir of Clovis, and then she was there not as prisoner at all but as the future queen. The household of Clovis was Christian; the future queen, it was decided, should be a Christian also, so they began to instruct her. There was order in that court, order and time and space and women did not mix too much with men, but lived in their own quarters and were treated it seemed to her at first with respect. She was introduced to God, and also to reading and writing and gracious arts. Their God became her god. Christ on the cross dying for her; his presence in the sacrament, in the bread and in the wine. In the singing, so different from the drunken brawlings of childhood; in the poetry and the carved wood, painted and gilded, that was turned into the statues of the saints. A God too whom you could talk with, in the quiet and privacy of your chamber, a God who listened to prayers rather than grew drunk on the blood of slaughtered animals.

All this was so lovely and comforting to her in her loneliness, that she accepted the other bits too. That women can unite with this God only through meekness and obedience; that women have a mission to bring sweetness to the lives of men; that wives must be obedient to their husbands, must keep silent, must honour and obey.

Obeying Clotaire as it turned out was a great deal easier than honouring him. He dealt with the obeying bit, with the back of his hand if all else failed. She struggled unaided with the honouring bit. She was eighteen when they were married and she came to her estate with a glowing heart. She knew he was a wild man, fierce and bloodthirsty and she believed that she could, in the power of Christ — and assisted by her beauty which even she knew, and knew with due modesty, was the kind that sets men's hearts aflame (and, as she learned quickly not just their hearts) — tame this man and make him loving and dutiful.

To this end she directed all her energies. It seemed to her that he devoted what energies he had to spare from pillage, massacre, and debauchery, to her humiliation. He threw her from her own bed at night so that he could lay his mistress there; he made her stand in the hall, in the presence of his war-band, while he berated her for her childlessness. He beat her. He mocked her. And, whenever he felt like it, without warning, without kindness, he raped her.

The priests around her muttered that this was but God's testing of her. She must accept all this in meekness for the glory of God and to save her husband's soul. He must be brought to see that her love was unwavering, that her forgiveness like Christ's was complete. Love would they assured her conquer all so long as she was strong in submission, was humble in humiliation, and was welcoming, warm, tender, sweet, good.

It was right they told her, even that he should interrupt her prayers because a woman came to God only through her husband; that her husband, her king, must be first for her, first even above God.

And she endured it. She believed them and she endured it.

Soft through the castle she went, silent and gentle. When he let her she was generous; and when he forbade it she consented. When he was away from her cavorting with his whores, with his friends, with his horses and hounds, she read and she prayed; when she heard that he was returning she put those things away and attended to his every whim. One day he would turn, one day he would turn and see her, see who she was, see this holy and gentle girl who made his needs her concern, who made his salvation the first matter of her intercession, who loved him and would suffer for and from him, turning her cheek as the Christ did, inviting him to smite the other side.

He killed her brother and made her watch.

He abused her body.

He laughed at her in public.

He burned her books.

She offered it up, she united her sufferings with the sufferings of Christ; she followed the instructions of St Paul and was obedient to him. One day, one day he would turn and love her; one day her long torture would be rewarded. If she were a good enough wife he would change. That was what God wanted. She was being tested. Clotaire and God were testing her. She had to endure in all meekness.

For six years, for six years she endured. She was, they said, as pious as she was beautiful. As good as she was lovely. She was a model of the Christian queen; she gave herself up to her husband's interests as a good woman should. For his political advantage she even consented to the death of her brother; she had left her father and her father's house and cleaved only to her husband in silence and in humility. She was a saint, they said, a banner of Christian womanhood in the dark north.

This did not comfort her.

One evening, late, he came to her chamber drunk, with a drunken comrade, arm in arm. 'Look at my lady wife,' he said with a laugh, 'get you a wife like this, friend. A wife who will do anything. A muling chicken, with the heart of a whore.'

And to her he said 'Take off your clothes.'

'No,' she said. She had not known she was going to say it. She had been ready, waiting, bathed and perfumed for him. She had thought this would be a night like any other. She was as startled as he was to hear her voice saying 'No'. To hear so calm and certain her own mouth say 'No'.

But once it was said, something changed.

She was a Thuringian fury, the dark power of the wild Viking gods of the north was on her; the strength and wrath of the God of the psalmist — the God who blighted Sodom in the night and laid low the walls of Jericho. The God who rode with David against the Philistines, and laid the seven curses on the children of Egypt.

The God who cleansed the temple.

While he stood there blankly, while his friend crept from the room, while his fury tried to gather itself and failed to overcome the stupor of his amazement, she started to speak.

'This, this,' she shouted, banging her own chest, 'this is a temple, a temple of the Holy Spirit, a house of God and you have made it a den of thieves. Enough. Do you hear me, enough. I don't care.'

He took a dazed step towards her and she snatched up the great glazed bowl that stood full of water on her armoire. She hurled it at him, and it crashed, a thousand splinters.

'And now I am leaving. In the morning. Arrange me transport. I am taking the veil, I am going to Noyons and they will make me a deaconess because of your noble name and then you will never be able to touch me again. Never.'

For one moment she saw in his eyes the thing she had debased herself for six years to see; a glimpse of awe, of respect, of admiration. But it was too late. What virtue had not gained her, anger had. What sweetness and suffering had failed to provide, anger did.

She heard the huge stern voice of Jesus saying to her as he had to Lazarus, 'Come out.' Come out of the grave and live.

When she rode away from her husband's house the next morning, setting forth boldly on the long road to Noyons, which would lead in due time to the shorter sunnier road to Poitiers and to her own foundation, her own daughters, her honour and power and glory she heard the cheers of Martha and Mary, and the Lady. She heard the laughter of Thecla, and the merriment of all the martyrs. She heard the voice of Jesus and was surprised but delighted to find that it did not, out from under the shadow of his high hall, sound remotely like the voice of Clotaire.

Life and love were strong and sweet. Her anger had made her a free woman. It was better to be gentle and good; order was better than chaos; peace and study than the wild nights of the war-bands. She was lucky because she was not just pious and beautiful, she was also clever and wise. She never questioned her luck; she never questioned God's kindness to her, but she never questioned the power of anger either. Our Lord in the temple, destroying the tables of the money-changers, is the same Lord as our Lord on the cross. Both.

Especially for women.

She wanted to tell the nuns that, here on this bright summer day, while she was dying. It seemed important.

She searched through her considerable resources of strength and determination. Then she knew that she did not have the time. They would have to learn it for themselves. They could look to her life and work it out.

The lavender-scented cloth moved tenderly across her face again. Fun, that is what she had had since leaving Clotaire. Happiness. Joy. Fun.

She smiled.

The nuns sang. She was ready now.

MARY FISHER

Mary Fisher, spinster, though not of this nor any other parish, was a vagabond woman, bound to the road as a husband is bound to house and home. She was never quite sure how this had come about.

She woke this morning cold and slightly shaky; the sky was paling and in the greyness the distant stars were extinguished one by one. The country had form but no colour. She stretched wearily and climbed out from under her rock — like a woodlouse, she thought, and smiled at so homely an image. Below her was the sea, as pale as the sky, milky, expectant, enormous. She waited, patient and pale as the stones at her feet.

When the sun rose out of the sea abrupt and bright, the world was flooded with colour like a miracle. On an instant as though out of its own substance, in response to the sun but not caused by it, the dry earth was golden brown, the sea and the sky together blue and gold and pink. She drew in a slow breath, wriggled her shoulders, shifting the stiffness, and as suddenly as the colour had come, as shocking and as surprising, so did happiness; she felt happy and free. She drew a handful of dried fruit from her sack and stuffed it into her mouth; she chewed into its roughness with great and simple pleasure, pushing her tongue against its hidden sweetness. Then she straightened her hair as best she could, turned her right shoulder to the vibrantly blue Aegean rocking its islands tenderly below her, and her left to the great mountains of Macedonia and Thrace curving down towards her, and started walking towards Adrianople again.

As she walked she listened and waited. But her inner voice was silent so that she could hear the first birds, the early song of the insects, the inaudible murmur of the sun warming rocks and dust and shrubby plants.

Later though she was vouchsafed a word: 'This is the day that the Lord has made; I will rejoice and be glad in it.'

So many mornings in ten years she had awakened in strange places. Mornings had come to her in many ways and many colours and still who could not rejoice, who could fail to feel the surge of hope, even when dawn caught one deep in a prison cell? In Boston the windows had been boarded over to protect the pious citizens from the contamination of her witchy presence, but even there, shadowed and nervous, the morning had come sneaking in, making its arrival known, creeping round every barrier, dispersing the horror of the night. She pushed Boston away quickly, concentrating on better times, on mornings in the Barbadoes where heat had come with the dawn, damp, strong smelling, potent; and on Pontefract where she had been shaped in the image of Christ, a prophet like him despised in her own town. In Selby too, in Cambridge, where she had had the honour to be the first of The Friends to be whipped, to be scourged as Christ was scourged, in York and in Virginia, she had been more than conqueror, empowered in a moment of her own choosing. And here, on the hard dry soil, she walked where no free-born English woman had ever walked before.

She had not expected to find the country itself so abundantly pleasing; the rockiness, the desert of it. Was it so in Holy Lands? Had the Saviour walked in his desert even as she did now? Had he smiled, as she did, to see the lizards skitter away, nervous and swift?

Yesterday had been different. Yesterday she had been given a different word:

> If God is for us, who is against us? What shall separate us from the love of God? Shall tribulation or distress or persecution or famine or nakedness or peril or sword? No, in all these things we are more than conquerors. For I am sure that neither death, nor life, nor angels, nor principalities, nor things present, nor things to come, nor powers, nor height, nor depth, nor anything else in all creation can separate us from the love of God?

'It is out of Paul, daughter,' she had heard her father's voice, far away, in time and place, her father's voice betraying her. 'It's out of Paul, daughter, a woman may not speak.'

He had betrayed her. Oliver had betrayed her. Love, hope, faith had betrayed her. The past, Paul had forgotten the past, things past can separate you from the love of God. Until yesterday betrayal had separated her from the love of God.

'I do not permit a woman to speak,' the cold minister had said, in front of all the congregation; 'Brother, take your daughter home and teach her respect. Respect for the word of God, and the good ordering of the Church.'

And even as they walked home she had continued to believe that as he had taught her, so he would justify her. 'I am a free-born Englishman,' he had said each morning of her childhood going out to seek for the work he would not find, 'I am a free-born Englishman; I plead the liberty of my conscience and I doff my hat to no man.'

She had been weaned on politics and religion. For her father with the authority of the Bible in his hand and the stirrings of change coming down on the wind from the north, would doff his hat to no man, nor let her curtsey ever. Such a small thing it seemed, but it was that she brought with her from the morning of knowledge; that she was free born and should doff her hat to no man. There had been other things, long ranting and shouting meetings, part Bible and part bile. There had been little gentleness in the making of the Commonwealth of God. But speeches full of predestination and covenants and taxes and prophecies and prayer books and parliaments make little impact on a small child. She had not understood that; what she had understood was the solid obduracy, the clear pride with which her father would keep his hat on his head, with which he would glare at her if he saw her knee so much as wobble, her head so much as nod, on the town street when the painted whores from the great houses who ground the faces of the children of God passed by. And as she grew, that obduracy cost him his work, his position, his comfort, his liberty and his ears, but not, oh never, his bell-like sense of himself as righteous, as justified, as proud, and as free born.

Inevitably, inevitably as the pulling of a tide or the waxing of the moon, he had marched off to join Cromwell's army and the only time in all her life that she saw love in his eyes was when he said the name *Oliver*.

She had trusted him and watched him go rejoicing, for his stubborn pride and his willingness to die for it, would bring in the Commonwealth of God. From his pride, and hers, the Kingdom would spring forth, the acceptable year of the Lord, the time of Jubilees; and their land would be called Beulah, because it was fruitful, and the spears and the swords would be beaten into pruning knives and ploughshares and each child of God Most High would sit under their own fruit tree in freedom and equality.

She had loved her father. She had loved the Lord Protector. 'Oliver, Oliver' they had shouted in the streets, and she with them. She had seen the light of the Spirit of Pentecost shine on his brow when he led the Lord's army out of the Fen Country with Liberty as his banner and Freedom of Conscience as his battle cry. Her father had marched with him, and she had nourished him in her prayers as the apple of her eye.

Under that glorious banner, and leading free-born men, he had ridden to Naseby and had fallen on the Man of Blood like the wave of the Red Sea that had fallen on Pharaoh and all the horses and chariots of the Egyptians. A wave had risen up in England that day, a wave of freedom and the riding of a tide of blood into the courts of the blasphemers. A tide of God, and filled with the Spirit, the army and the children of freedom had prophesied the coming of the Kingdom and rejoiced.

Oliver had taught them freedom. He had taught them in the Assemblies how to argue, how to understand the word of God when it came to the ruling of the nation of God; he taught them how to stand up and doff their hats to no man. Then he betrayed them.

He used them to winnow Parliament; to put down the King and to throw out the papish prayer book. He used them to set himself up in the King's place; to abuse the rights of Parliament; and to impose the preaching of the presbyters. He gave them neither liberty nor freedom of conscience and said the land could not be ruled by those who had neither property nor interest.

Oliver had snatched her father in his pride and sent him home defeated. Oliver had betrayed him; and he betrayed her.

'I do not permit a woman to speak,' the cold minister had said, in front of all the congregation; 'Brother, take your daughter home and teach her respect. Respect for the word of God, and the good ordering of the Church.'

And even as they walked home she had continued to believe

that as he had taught her, so he would justify her. He drank sullenly all evening and she sat at the table waiting on his words. Late, late in the night, her waiting came finally to an end. He stood up. 'I'll not have you shame me,' he said wearily. She said nothing.

'It's out of Paul, daughter, a woman may not speak.'

She did not, but slowly she rose too, the pair of them facing each other across the room.

'You lack respect,' he said, still in that tired voice.

'I plead the Freedom of my Conscience,' she said calmly. 'As you taught, I'll doff my hat to no man.'

So he beat her.

He went out the next morning ashamed, leaving before dawn while she lay still on the floor. Later she got up, washed as best she might, changed her torn dress and ordered her hair. Then she left the house and never returned, because she knew her love for him would betray her if he pleaded with her.

Soon afterwards she heard Elizabeth Hooton preach and she joined herself to The Friends. She was moved to do so because they let women preach and stood for Freedom of Conscience against all the principalities of the world. They held all people free-born children of God and set no one in authority over another.

In the power of the inner light she had become a vagabond, preaching and proclaiming — in York, in Selby, in Cambridge, in Boston, in Virginia, in the islands of the Carib Indians, the Barbadoes.

'I am led,' she had told the York meeting, 'I am led to cross the seas again; I have heard a clear call to go and preach to him whom the world calls the Sultan, the Emperor of the Pagans.'

The meeting had not been unduly surprised, and why should they have been? They did not question her call, nor she theirs to stay at home. They made such preparations as they could and prayed her on her journey.

But she had not been called; she had been driven. Driven by the need to go away; to flee from all the places of childhood and safety, to trust no one and nothing for fear of betrayal.

Then, yesterday she had been vouchsafed a word; and walking all day alone, walking in anger and resentment and loneliness she had come to realize that Paul had left something out of his list.

It was the past, the past had separated her from the love of God. She turned, she turned to the past, and in the turning — in hearing the weariness of her father's voice, the sadness of defeat, the loss of hope, of faith that must of itself bring in the loss of love — she took up her past and saw that it had made her who she was. Led and driven were not different ways; they were different responses. If she had walked in love and forgiveness she would have walked the same road as she had walked in pain and bitterness — she would just have had more fun. More joy.

> He who has dipped his hand in the dish with me, will betray me. The Son of Man goes as it is written of him, but woe to the man by whom the Son of Man is betrayed.

She wept for her father. His woe was greater than hers. She forgave him. After all, she liked being a vagabond woman.

In this new understanding she rose at dawn; and with the flooding of world in the light, she thought 'This is the day that the Lord has made; I will rejoice and be glad in it.'

She walked all that day, beginning at last the long descent into the great fertile valley where Europe and Asia meet, and was sorry that she had wasted so much time hating. For betrayal had led her to this land of loveliness.

A few weeks later she walked into the great palace of Adrianople and became the first Christian woman to preach to the Sultan. When she was about to enter the presence, a courtier handed her a veil and indicated that she should cover her face and kneel on the ground before him. She almost giggled when she refused, saying 'I must plead the Liberty of my Conscience, for I am a free-born woman and doff my hat to no man.' The courtier looked both confused and terrified but she was filled with gaiety.

So when the Sultan, sitting composed and magnificent on his silken cushions, raised his head — his court prostrate, their faces covered, before him — he looked for the first time in his life into a pair of level eyes that showed neither fear nor desire. He smiled at her. He was only eighteen.

> If God is for us, who is against us? What shall separate us from the love of God? Shall tribulation or distress or persecution or famine or nakedness or peril or sword? No in all these things we are more than conquerors. For I am sure

that neither death, nor life, nor angels, nor principalities, nor things present, nor things past nor things to come, nor powers, nor height, nor depth, nor anything else in all creation can separate us from the love of God.

We are free, she told him, if we can believe this and go on loving, in the power of the light within us. Woe is for the betrayer, not the betrayed.

'Yes, that is true,' he repeated more than once — if the cautious interpreter really repeated their words to one another honestly.

The important thing was the smile that they had shared.

MARGARET CLITHEROW

ᏒᎬᎬᏒ

'Margaret', 'Margaret, Maggie', 'Maggie', 'Mother', 'Madam', 'Mistress Clitherow', 'Meg', 'Mama', 'Meggie'. They call her from sleep, and she surfaces reluctantly.

Margaret, Mother, Maggie, Meg, and from far away, distant, almost inaudible — Mouse, little Mouse, daddy's little Mousie Mouse.

She is only just thirty; she is young to have so many names, so many voices calling. She will not accumulate any more.

They wake her to tell her, to ask her, to beg her, to plead.

Jesus was silent and made no answer.

She has not, she will not, she is not going to plead. 'Having made no offence I need no trial.' She holds on to that against the voices of her dreams, and against the real voices. They are not angry voices, they are respectful, friendly, supportive, loving. That makes it so much harder.

In the martyrologies, the stories, the histories it is never like this. Against a wicked emperor, against a rough soldier, against a man who wants to have his way with you, it is easy to be stubborn.

But here.

'Mistress Clitherow, you must answer to this court,' says Justice Clinch, and then breaking down, '. . . for heaven's sake, Maggie, plead. Please.' That is not how the mighty and powerful, the cruel emperor, the wicked civil servant should speak. It is how your friends speak. And it makes it very difficult. Because they are all together, she and John and Justice Clinch and Justice Rhodes and all the others. They danced round the maypole together; they were young together, young and a cut above the more humble citizens of York. They were Justices now and John was a chamberlain and her father had been Sheriff; and they have fine houses in the Shambles with heavy wooden beams and white paint and carved staircases. She was with Mistress Clinch when she gave birth to little Jamie Clinch. She petted Annie Clinch's finger when she shut it in the big linen kist. Justice Clinch does not want to order her to be pressed: the *peine forte et dure*, the slow pressing to death under a weighted board, the punishment for a refusal to plead. She is waking here this morning in the cool shadows of the prison because Justice Clinch and Justice Rhodes have given her time to change her mind — have given all the people who love her one more chance to get at her.

And she likes him so much. He is a good man, pushed against a wall of the Law as heavy as the pressing board. She is tempted, tempted to make his life easier.

'Margaret.' William wants her to plead too. For very different reasons. Father William, she knows, and knows affectionately, is jealous. He does not really approve of women being martyrs; they should stay at home and take care of priests like him, until the moment comes for their heroic deaths, defending the faith. So poor William is put about. She was after all his convert; not a Catholic born, not like him — and it does not seem quite fair that she a woman, a wife, the wife of a Protestant, the mother of a happy brood of lively children, lively, witty, happy, should nonetheless sneak into heaven before him. But if she is going to be a martyr, Father William thinks, she should do it properly.

She should plead, she should plead guilty; she should, like blessed Richard Thirkeld, appearing in court in priest's cassock and biretta, make a big wonderful disputation, and controversing with the Dean himself. She should do it like that, a fine and high statement of the glorious truth, teaching the Geneva boys the folly of their ways, from the writings of the Fathers. The fact that she, Margaret Middleton, wife of John Clitherow, butcher and chamberlain, only learned to read while she was in prison the last time and has never read a word of the Fathers of the Church, nor cares to, seems to have escaped him. Now he is worried that all her penances and mortifications and the clarity of the charge and her long record of encouraging Catholics and harbouring priests and the evidence against her will not be enough. If she will not plead guilty, then she will die for defiance of the court, not for the sake of the Gospel. Will she be a martyr then? Will he have been the director of the soul of a saint? It would make up for the fact that he failed to get himself arrested, that he had allowed her to bundle him into the priest hole, and left her and her outrageous family to deal with the pursuivants. He wants, he needs her to do it properly. She is tempted, tempted to give him his fierce desire.

Jesus was silent and made no answer.

'Meggie.' Her mother does not understand. 'You have to plead in a court house,' she says plaintively, 'you have to. Everyone says you have to.' She is worried again, still, that somehow Margaret is not behaving properly, that she did not bring her daughter up right. 'I tried,' she says to Margaret now, 'I did try.' She is old, but her whining still grates. 'I taught you properly and I married you well,' she moans, 'didn't I teach you properly?'

'Yes, mother,' she says, offering it up a little desperately. 'Yes, you did. It's not your fault, you brought me up so strictly in the established Protestant religion that I did not suspect there was any other way to serve God.'

'You should do what John tells you,' begs her mother, 'he's a good man. Isn't he a good man? Poor John. What he has to put up with. You ought to do what your husband tells you. John says you should plead. It's not fair on Mr Rhodes. It's not fair on me . . . what will people say? . . . poor John . . . the children . . . me, me, me . . . it's not my fault . . . I brought you up as best I could . . . what would your father say? . . .'

'I'll ask him in heaven, if he got there.' She did not say it. She bit her lip and tried to shut out the low whingeing of her mother's aged grumblings. Her father had died, when she was very young, and had left her a silver goblet and six silver spoons for her inheritance. How could it matter what he would say now? Far away, in some lost place of her dream world, she can smell his huge body, feel the rough tickle of his beard, his great hug in the hall way of their town house, 'Where's my mouse, my little mousie mouse?', his great voice booming warm and strong through the fine timbers of his house. She is tempted to turn back into that hug, into the approval of everything she was brought up to honour and respect.

It is one more sound she tries to shut out. She tries to concentrate.

'Having made no offence, I need no trial.'

Jesus was silent and made no answer.

'Mother', Henry in Douai, William longing to go; 'Mama', Anne, little John, Katherine. They do not ask her to plead. They do not ask for anything except that none of this should be happening. She should come home. She should be laughing, their great house should be filled with happy laughter, the apprentices kicking their heels and teasing the little girls, the school room should be full of little ones, and upstairs some poor scared priest on the run, off the moors with a cough on his chest, should be saying his office inside the curtains of the big bed and looking forward to breakfast. It is exciting when the priests come; and the boys slide down the long bannister; and their father comes into the hall and shouts for quiet and his wife; and she comes running from school room, or still room, or nursery and the children know that although their parents agree about nothing, they in truth agree about everything — about all the important things — that a house should be warm and hospitable and full of laughter and singing and helping each other and cuddling and learning and blessing. They think they can stop it all, they think she will come home and everything will be all right, and they are too young to know that it is too late.

The *peine forte et dure*. It will give them nightmares. But better than the other nightmares. That temptation is easier to resist.

Mm . . . Mm . . . mmmm . . . says the little one inside her. The one she must not listen to, the one whose sole hope she is, the one who will never get a chance . . . the one who is the only thing in the world that will turn John's love from her, because she is killing his child too, for her stubbornness.

'Meg.' No martyr of the early Church; no priest strung up at York Tyburn on the tree that is the door to heaven, no hero of the faith that she has ever read about or heard about or prayed for or prayed to has had to answer for their faith before such a judge — husband, lover, friend, man of good will and kindness and passion, and ah such yearning, desiring, loving — saying 'Meg, dear heart please, plead. We might get you off. We might. Meg, for love's sake, my dear child, my lovebird, my sweet love, for my sake, plead.'

Jesus was silent and made no answer.

'Having made no offence, I need no trial.' But it comes out

as a whimper and she knows the harshness in our Lord's voice
when he said to Peter 'Get thee behind me'. It is not anger, it is
the melting, the tender melting of love that makes such an appeal
such a threat to her stubborn will. She tries to persuade him he
is wrong, that she will die anyway, but he is so full of life and
hope and honour.

'We got you off the last time.'

'I'm still on bail . . . failure to attend the parish, that's a
little thing. But massing stuff, John, they found it. Ah, that
poor boy, John, be gentle with him.'

'They threatened him. It was evidence under threat of violence. That is not allowed. And he's Flemish, they threatened
him and he could not understand them properly. I will argue.
They don't want to, the Justices, they don't want to convict
you Meg; give them a chance. Plead not guilty and we'll have
a chance. You have to.' He lays his hand on her stomach. He
will not mention the baby, he is too clean and decent to use it,
but he cannot restrain his loving hand, his need to touch her and
touch his child inside her.

'It's my turn, Meg. Everything, everything you have wanted I
have done. My house full of criminals, my bed empty on a Friday
and goodwives preferring the meat of other butchers. William
has gone to Douai, and Henry will go too and Anne for a nun I
dare say, but please, be fair, you have to give something. Your
church cannot ask this of you.'

'It won't work, Johnnie,' she says softly, leaning on him
now. 'It won't work, because I would not be me.' She knows
now, for prayer does help you learn the truth, that she had
become a Catholic at nineteen because she wanted to have
something that was not his, she wanted something for herself; but she had never meant to let that take away from
him. She did not know that it would become who she was;
that not to go through this now, though she had not sought
and did not choose it, would make her not the woman that
he loved, would make her someone else. Harbouring priests,
a felony, a treason. It was not that, it was more simple. She
had to stand to herself so that she could lean on him and
weep because she could not give him this thing, this little
thing that he asked her for, he who asked for so little, she
could not give it to him and still be the person who made his

eyes fill with begging tears although he was a strong and good man.

It is this tough thing that is between them. When two people meet as equals in a world where they are not meant to do so, each must have a hard tough thing of their own. She knows this. She cannot tell him because he will not understand. She can only follow the wisdom of heart, believe that she will be saved by the truth, and hope that he will be saved by God's mercy, although the priests do not think so.

'Why?' he says at last. 'Why won't you plead?'

'I cannot ask the children, the maid girls, the apprentices to witness against me, and I cannot ask them to perjure themselves. It is simple. I cannot do that to them. It would . . . it would . . . damage them. John, do you remember . . . ?'

He does, and he understands. When they were young, before they were married, they had gone to watch a witch trial. And the witch's daughter had given witness against her mother. So much pain, so much pain in both their faces. And three weeks later, courting by the river side, they had found the daughter, her face bloated from the river, dead by her own hand, dead and damned, so she might as well have gone for a witch and not known the pain of that betrayal.

'I cannot, John. I love them. You weren't in the house, and you cannot bear witness against your wife. It will have to be them, and I cannot. I will not plead.'

He looks away embarrassed. He had not thought of so much love. There is a hardness in her, there has always been, and her penancing and popish folly and mortification have made it harder still. But the hardness is another name for an enormous softness, a cradling that has made all her stupidity and stubbornness a gift to him.

He does not agree, but he consents, as he has always done, not because he is weak but because he sees and understands a strength in her that would make anything else an insult. He looks at her slowly, half grinning like a little boy caught out with a stolen sweetmeat in his mouth, and he says 'Having made no offence you need no trial.' Then, after a pause, he says sadly 'I will not tell them, Meg; if you can do that for them, then I can keep quiet for them too.'

'Thank you,' she says.

Then, because everything is dealt with now, he laughs and says 'You will try to teach me that you are such a good mother because Mary has come and taught you how.'

She laughs too and says 'I shall be rude to them in court today. I shall try to make them angry. I want it to be today.'

He looks startled, because she is so clear.

'Why?' he asks.

'This Friday,' she says, 'is my day. How often, how often in all history do the Annunciation and Good Friday happen on the same day? March 25th, in the year of our Lord fifteen hundred and eighty-six. God be thanked, I am not worthy of so good a death as this.'

'That's a fine and handsome line, Meg, my lovely,' he says trying not to weep at the purity of the child who will go to heaven showing off; struggling to match her flowing laughter, her golden joy, 'a good line; be sure to say it in your last speech.'

And because she loved him she did.

PERPETUA AND FELICITY

〆ᲽᲽᲽ

Vibia Perpetua is twenty-two years old. She is nursing her first baby. When he cries her breasts respond, magically, which is both satisfying and embarrassing. He feeds on her body, and he helped her understand. When she is away from him for more than a couple of hours her breasts grow hard and heavy, even painful. He needs her, and she therefore needs him, he has helped her understand. When she feeds him she feels a strange tingling as the milk lets down and she watches his eager loving lips suckle and she is enchanted. She loves her son, ignores her husband, respects her mother and hates her father. She is beautiful, nobly born, highly articulate and very well educated. She is used to being admired and getting her own way; but despite this she is often frightened. When she is frightened she becomes more articulate than ever, protecting her fear — which she despises — with a brightness and a certainty which others find convincing. If you like her you say that she has natural leadership potential, or what a pity she was born a girl. If you don't like her you say she is a spoiled brat, or a bossy show-off. When she knows that the stage is set for her own martyrdom she thinks, rightly, that she is very young to die, but also, rightly, that she will look stunning in the arena.

Felicity is different. Felicity is silent. Silent and sullen. Obstinate. There comes a point, she has come to believe, where words are impossible, where everyone else takes them over and leaves you none. There comes a point where only sullenness will work, only silence will pay. A place where the sulking child has to take over from the grown woman. The grown woman has learned that you have to try and please Them. But you come at last to a place where the grown woman has to lean on the mute strength of the sulking child who knows that They can yell at you, that They can beat you, that They can punish and even kill you, but They cannot make you consent, cannot make you obey. They cannot make you smile. There comes a space, a time, when you just have to hunker down in grim silence, not answer back, not try to explain, not respond, just live in the immovable heavy power of your own silence. It will be enough, just, and it will be everything.

Felicity is pregnant with a child she does not want. She has stepped outside the condition of her own slavery to proclaim her own freedom to believe in a God in whom there will be neither slave nor free, male nor female. It has been an enormous effort laying claim to new possibility. She comes to her imprisonment already exhausted, worn out by slavery, pregnancy and freedom. She has to burrow into the inside of her own silence and hug herself there. There is nothing else.

Their story is essentially very simple. They found something, heard it in the breezes in the market place, in the soft philosophical dialogues, in the songs of men and women at the well sides, in the irritation of the Roman civil service. A warm scent on a soft wind out of the east, whence truth tends to come; it stirred the sands of the desert stretching south towards the sun, and it murmured to them of something they needed. In whispers, at first, and later in excited shouts, they searched and found a group of people who were lit up, vibrantly alive in the knowledge that God had called their names and set them free, and shared himself and his food with them regardless. Despite doubts and despite warnings they joined themselves with these groups. They called themselves Christians. They started to learn what that might mean.

They are arrested with other catechumens — other trainee Christians, receiving pre-baptismal instruction — during the persecution of Septimius Severus who has forbidden fresh conversions to this inconvenient faith. This makes the catechumens, but them alone, liable to the death penalty. Quite crafty actually; and a monument to Roman pragmatism which believes in freedom of worship but which cannot cope with a sect that laughs at the Empire. So they, with others, are arrested, imprisoned, tried, found guilty and made to wait for sentencing. The waiting is to give them a chance to change their minds. A recantation is, surprisingly, an even better deterrent to those tempted by the rebellious teachings of this sect than a persecution.

No one in authority actually wants to have them killed: Christians tend not to provide much amusement in the arena, they are brave, but passive; offering neither the amusements of terror nor those of bold struggle. In any case there are plenty of more appropriate gladiators. They are shoved into dark and uncomfortable cells, slightly overcrowded and slightly underfed, and their families are encouraged to visit them and talk to them of all the pleasures of life and make them feel foolish and guilty for inflicting such pain on all who love them. It does sometimes work, although it soon becomes clear that with this particular group of catechumens it is not going to.

Perpetua keeps a journal. It is not altogether honest. She knows that it will not be read until after her death, until after she has become a martyr and saint of the Church. It will be a testament of her passion; it will be read in the little congregations along the Mediterranean coast and up in Greece and the islands, even perhaps in Jerusalem. She knows this so clearly that, although she means to be honest, she cannot avoid a certain self-consciousness, a certain reconstruction of herself so that she looks like a martyr and saint of the Church. She knows, for instance, that she did not speak to her father with quite the bold certainty, the high-handed impertinence, the elegant wit that she records. She knows that when they took her son away her breasts ached and dripped and spoiled her tunic until Felicity bound them tightly with a long linen headpiece. She does not know if the child cried and whimpered through the night, his lips working plaintively for the tit he cannot find. But somehow tearful sulkiness and damp soggy patches down her front do not shape the narrative in the direction she would choose. She wants there to be some point to her sad demise, and the point will be the edification of Christians throughout the Empire who really will not be too interested in the inconveniences of sudden weaning.

She also leaves things out when she cannot quite understand them: she was appalled when the rest of them agreed with Felicity that they should pray for a premature labour. Perpetua, despite her boldness, is a daughter of the ruling élite, she cannot but feel that children are precious, are the future, even the children of slaves. She cannot but feel that Felicity does not have the right to risk the life of her child just in order to get martyred.

She is secretly rather proud of the fact that the Empire is too civilized to send pregnant women to the arena. Even more secretly she would rather like to be the only woman in the expedition.

Moreover she finds the whole thing rather vulgar. Noisy prayer, and a certain amount of wine, oil and emetic, followed by that screamingly painful public labour, with the guards laughing and the companions shouting advice, that can have been learned only in brothels and bars. And when finally she gives in and offers her womanly, and it must be said experienced, support to a slave girl, she is rejected. Felicity, panting and sweaty, turns her head away, pushes Perpetua aside and clings to the hand of Saturninus, a huge crude cowardly man, in Perpetua's opinion, and clamps a fold of his shirt front between her teeth.

She has, moreover, a strong sense that Felicity does not like her, that Felicity sees through her and in the depths of her sulky little mind may very well be laughing at her, at her, Vibia Perpetua. She knows she should be able to handle this with humility or with serenity, and she cannot. So these things do not get recorded in Perpetua's journal, although she knows they should be. She just does not know how to record them.

About the dreams though, about the extraordinary and powerful dreams, she is honest. Like her companions she knows that dreams do not belong to the dreamer but to God. They are angelic messages and she records them with care.

She walks in heaven, beside the great fountain. She embraces her beloved baby brother, the son who died leaving her as her father's substitute. She loved him, and he died and now he is waiting for her in heaven.

She strips naked, as He was stripped and climbs a dangerous ladder, as He climbed. Her companions surround her receiving her clothing, they oil and cream her body for the great fight. Now she has become man, a warrior, a hero; now she goes out to wrestle with a great Egyptian devil monster; now she rises high in the air above him, and smites him with her heels and dances on his broken head, and there is great rejoicing and they all know that they are privileged and have been found worthy to join their Lord in the great act of witness, in passion and in death. She records the dreams with great precision, struggling to capture not just the words but the precise feeling of them. Even here she knows that she does not get it quite right, but so perseveres, because it is important.

For three weeks they are in prison. Perpetua and Felicity kneel back to back in the darkness while everything is taken away from them. Their children are taken away: Perpetua's by her doting family, Felicity's by the unloving guards. The one thing Perpetua truly loved, the one thing Felicity truly hated. There is nothing in the new space, except the dark. There is nothing except their resistance to each other. No, no they will not, they will not give up their anger and dislike. They will not move towards each other. It is their last claim, their last resistance, their last privilege. The privilege not to deal with each other, not to deal with the difference and darkness and dislike that is there in class and style and determination and desire. They resist. They refuse. Perpetua dreams her dreams and declares her visions. Heaven and hell are open to her now and her companions receive her gifts with gratitude. She knows that Felicity will have no part in this; that Felicity walks her own silent road, not singing and dancing and performing, but battening down the hatches to endure and to endure and to endure. Felicity clings equally to her own secrecy; she knows that Perpetua is scared, is terrified, she knows that Perpetua clings to her dreams and her authority in order not to have to face that fear; and she hates her, she hates the brightness and the belatedness, she hates the ease of authority and the knowing. She hates the beauty and brains. She clings to her silence and her hatred and neither will comfort the other.

The night before they died something changes. It begins, rightly, with a joke. Saturninus, suddenly, unexpectedly, like a child, admits that he is scared of bears. He is horrified, appalled, terrified, rendered senseless and trembling, by bears. He knows absolutely that he cannot die bravely if he is obliged to confront a bear. What can he do? They pray a leopard for him. They pray not simply for a not-bear, but quite specifically for a leopard. For his peace of mind and for their honour they ask God to let him be killed by a spotty cat. And it makes them laugh.

Somewhere in the laughter, in the silliness and sadness of it all, Perpetua and Felicity find each other. Because nothing matters any more, or because everything does. Or both.

The next morning they march into the arena as friends, holding hands, united in love and triumph. They are singing, and their songs are the songs of freedom and friendship. 'We came here willingly,' says Perpetua for both of them, and she has been practising this speech in her head for three weeks. 'We came here willingly, so that our liberty might not be obscured.' We are free, she says, while their post-partum, lactating, dripping women's bodies cause an unwelcome disturbance to the ogling crowd. 'For this cause, for freedom and liberty, we have dedicated our lives. This is our contract with the law.'

'We have come here willingly, so that our freedom may not be obscured.'

Freedom, Felicity knows but does not say, freedom consists of voices that have been broken and blood that has been spilled. Freedom tastes of pain.

The animals are prepared for the killing: bears — though not for Saturninus who is dispatched, singing, by a finely spotted leopard — bears and wild cats and boars. And a mad cow for women, as is appropriate. The mad cow tosses them, but holding hands they help each other to their feet. This is love, love and freedom, sing their battered bodies, this is a love that no one can take from us. Perpetua is so wrapped up in excitement and ecstasy that she does not even notice the flesh torn by the cow's horn. Felicity smiles. Now they have come to this new place Felicity thinks it funny and rather sweet that Perpetua should still be interested in ecstasy.

In the end they are led, still singing, to the place of execution. They exchange a kiss. It is called the kiss of peace, but for both of them now it is a kiss of love and anticipation.

Their throats are cut.

Felicity, stubborn to the last, consents to die.

Perpetua, flamboyant to the last, insists on assisting her incompetent and pain-inflicting executioner with his job. She points with her elegant manicured fingers to the precise point in her neck where the axe-man should aim his blow. At the very final moment she knows she cannot look at Felicity's severed head, at Felicity's still-twitching decapitated trunk, so she has to talk. It is painful for the poor young executioner and she recognizes this without guilt. Her last wish is that she were brave enough not to have to score points off a conscripted youth's social shame, brave enough not to have to show off. It is too late even for that.

It is finished. They bleed to death on the hot sand of the circus.

&⸲&

All the five women in this series are real historical persons.

Lady Godiva lived in Coventry at the time of the Norman conquest — she, and her husband, are mentioned in the Domes- day Book, and her now legendary naked ride through the city, in order to win a tax rebate for the citizens, is recorded as early as 1150. As a footnote her will contains the first reference to the rosary in England, for there is a bequest of the 'circle of jewels for the Lady's prayers' in it.

Radegund (518–587) left her remarkably — even for the sixth century — vicious husband, King Clotaire of the Franks, and founded the convent of the Holy Cross at Poitiers. It became famous as a centre of scholarship and the arts.

Mary Fisher was born in 1623; in 1652 she joined the Society of Friends (the Quakers) which had been founded by George Fox and Elizabeth Hooton in about 1646. She quickly became a recog- nized preacher, working in England, Boston and the Caribbean, and finally setting out on her long journey to preach to the Sultan of the Ottoman Empire, Mohammed IV. After she returned to England she married, and later, as a widow, married a second time and emigrated to Carolina where she remained, active into her seventies.

Margaret Clitherow (1555/56–86) is one of the three women among the 'Forty Martyrs of England and Wales' canonized in 1970. The indictment against her was that she had harboured priests, which was a major felony under Elizabeth. Her refusal to plead at all, because she did not wish her children and servants to have to bear witness against her, meant that she was automatically subject to the *peine forte et dure* — the slow squashing to death under a heavy board. This punishment for non-participation in one's own trial was carried out in England until 1741. In 1772 the law was changed, so that a person refusing to plead was treated as guilty and punished accordingly. In 1826 Statute law directed that a prisoner refusing to plead, unless insane, was to be treated as though they had pleaded not guilty, and their trial proceeded in the normal way. Margaret's husband was, and continued to be, a Protestant, but always allowed his wife the liberty of her own faith.

Perpetua and Felicity were martyred in Carthage in AD 203. Perpetua's account of her arrest, imprisonment and visions, with an added description of their deaths in the arena — entitled *The Passion of Perpetua and Felicity* — was an important document to the early Church: and now it provides some of the earliest information we have about the experience of Christians in the post-apostolic era. It also gives us, first hand, the strong and individual voice of an early Christian woman. Perpetua and Felicity were named in the pre-conciliar rite of the Roman Catholic Mass.

ANGEL AND ME

❧❀❧

TRIUMPHANT ENTRY

Last weekend I went for a walk. It was a very long walk actually. I had planned for it to be quite a long walk, but one of my problems in life is that I tend to get over-enthusiastic about things. I have to say that I think this is one of my more endearing personality traits, although not everyone would agree. My family don't agree anyway. When I said 'How about a nice long walk this afternoon?' the suggestion was met somewhat negatively. In fact totally negatively, so I went for the walk on my own.

And I underestimated the distance and then somehow I managed to get lost, and quite tired, and anyway I wasn't wearing completely sensible shoes, and the weather wasn't very nice. And just at the point that my temper was beginning to feel frayed at the edges my guardian angel put in an appearance.

Well, I should have known she would. It's absolutely typical. You sit around in church praying like mad for hours on end and you don't get a cheep out of them. You get out of bed extra early in order to wash and iron the particular skirt that your daughter suddenly insists she absolutely has *to have for school; and when your sons ask where their socks are you refrain from telling them sharpish that they are probably exactly where they left them.*

The point I'm trying to make is that here you are being unselfish and sweet and maternal and good, and does your guardian angel turn up to observe this virtue, or even congratulate you? No, she does not. Or at least mine *does not — she lurks about furtively, waiting for the moment when my damp shoe starts to rub a blister in my heel and it becomes entirely apparent that despite all my promises I'm not going to get home in time to take my youngest son out to buy his new track suit and then,* then, *I get the usual old twitchy feeling just above my coccyx, followed by that odd sort of warm glow up my spinal column and there she is materializing somewhere in the region* of the *corpus callosum*. (Just in case you don't know, the *corpus callosum* is the bit that connects your right brain with your left brain and enables them to communicate their different skills to each other. And I do have to say that I think it is a bit sinister that my guardian angel often locates herself just there so that I can never be quite sure if I'm dealing with a rational, objective, verbal perception, or an imaginative, fluid, musical one.)

Anyway to get on with the story, here I was on my walk and my Angel turned up.

'Hello,' she said in her faintly glottal-stopped accent, 'you do look sweaty.'

I mean to say . . . there might have been a very different outcome to salvation history if Gabriel had burst in on Mary and said 'Hi, pity about the spot on your nose, but nonetheless do you want to be the mother of God?' I said as much to Angel actually, but she just smiled benignly and said 'The Queen of Heaven never suffered from acne.'

She sounded as though she had just read this in whatever the angelic equivalent of a women's magazine article about Princess Di is. I don't want you to think I'm a snob or anything like that, but it is disappointing to discover that angels can be extremely common: fascinated by royalty and with rather down-market accents, if you know what I mean. It makes me wonder about heaven.

'What do you want?' I asked. Rather ungraciously I admit.

'Well,' she replied, 'I thought I might encourage you to take a little rest.'

'I'll be late,' I said crossly. I found it a bit difficult to believe that she was really concerned about my physical comfort. That didn't seem very spiritual really. I rather feared I was about to get a little lecture on something or other.

'You're late already,' she commented. Not very helpfully, I thought. But I stopped and propped myself against a handy gate.

'Actually,' she said, 'I was rather hoping that I could persuade you to be honest about that lateness.'

'I wasn't going to lie!' I said, outraged. It was true that I had thought that I might bring the bull I had seen in a distant field a bit nearer, and possibly deepen the puddle into which I had splashed into something more closely approximating a pot-hole. But I wasn't going to *lie*.

'No?' said Angel. 'Well, that's all right then.'

You may be getting the impression that Angel and I don't always get on terribly well. You would be right. I don't know what I've done to deserve it, but I have the most unsatisfactory guardian angel in the cosmos. It really isn't just the women's magazine opinions and the rather ugly accent. She is almost unbelievably tedious and always concerned with the most mundane of ethical issues. You read about Jacob's ladder, or St Teresa of Avila's trances and you can't help but wonder if God is still up to the job. At the very least you expect a bit of glamour.

This was precisely what I felt as I leaned against my gate, tired, damp and, as she had so rightly but unkindly noted, sweaty.

'Look,' I said, a bit aggressively, 'I'm fed up. I've worked and worked on this prayer business' — this was a bit of an exaggeration really but I wanted to get my point across — 'and it's high time I got something out of it. I want a mystical vision.'

'Please,' she said.

'What?' I replied.

'You should say "please". You should say "I want a mystical vision, please." That's what you say to *your* children.'

Which is a perfect example of exactly the sort of thing I'm complaining about. However I didn't want to pick a fight just then so I intoned 'I want a mystical vision, please.'

'You've got me,' she said, and I felt she said it smugly.

'What?!'

'You've got me. I *am* a mystical vision. I am an actual and sensible presence of God manifested to you by divine grace.'

'Oh, for heaven's sake,' I muttered.

'Precisely,' she said. Then there was a bit of a pause and it dawned on me rather nastily that I might have hurt her feelings.

'I apologize,' I said, a bit huffily.

'That's OK,' she said, and I must say she didn't sound at all huffy, 'I apologize too, for being impatient. It's just that sometimes I can't help wondering what I've done to deserve it. I mean, having the most unsatisfactory client in the cosmos.'

There was another pause during which I refused to feel guilty. Then she said 'All right then. What sort of mystical vision do you have in mind?'

To be honest I was entirely taken aback.

'I don't really know,' I stumbled, 'what can you do?'

'*My* limitations', she said primly, 'are unlikely to prove the problem.'

I have to say that I didn't care for her tone. I replied with as much dignity as I could muster, 'You cannot seriously expect me to believe that God would let a junior angel do just anything: I mean levitation, stigmata, mystical marriage, the big time . . . .'

'What', she said coolly, 'makes you think I am a junior angel?'

I didn't want to hurt her feelings and by now I really did want a mystical vision. So I tried for some pretty bogus humility, which usually pleases her.

'Oh, I wouldn't have thought that a senior angel would be wasted on an unworthy, amateurish soul like me.'

It did not have the desired effect. Quite the contrary in fact.

There was a dazzling flare of light between my eyes; I thought I would be blinded by the glory. I saw the battle in heaven when the tail of the great dragon swept a third of all the stars from the heavens, and cast them into the vast emptiness of hell. I heard the roaring of thunder in the pinions of Angel's huge and powerful wings. The ground shook beneath my feet, and darkness covered the face of the earth. The sun and moon reeled in their courses and I felt a sharp pain between the top of my legs and the bottom of my back exactly as though someone had kicked me, hard. I saw and felt the fullness of heavenly wrath.

'What was that for?' I said crossly, as soon as I could breathe properly.

'*Never say that again*,' she said, and I have never heard her sound like that. 'Never,' she repeated sternly. 'If you do not know your own preciousness, then at least have the simple good manners not to suppose that He would have wasted His valuable and divine time on anything amateurish and unworthy. The cheek of it.'

I was about to protest loudly and give her a little lecture on humility and modesty, when I found that I had a lump in my throat and my eyes had gone all wet. Presumably from the shock and from the rain. I stopped leaning on the gate and started to walk down the hill at high speed. She wouldn't go away though.

She came with me down the hill, and through the next gate which led onto a lane that I recognized. I turned towards home and she came with me. You can't exactly out-run a determined angel. She came with me. After about fifteen minutes I was exhausted. I was wet and cold and miserable.

'Hey,' she said, at last, and she sounded so gentle. 'It's all right. I forgot how much it hurts you humans the first time you learn about being loved. Odd really. I'm sorry.'

I didn't answer. I couldn't as a matter of fact. I just walked on. The rain stopped and a weak wet sun appeared. I felt a bit better. But Angel didn't go away; she lurked, discreetly but defiantly.

After a little while longer she said, sounding more like herself, 'What about this mystical vision, then?'

'I don't want one,' I said, sulkily like a child.

'Well, you're going to get one anyway,' she said, with a total return to her usual bossy manner. 'You might even enjoy it now.'

I was about to engage in a healthy debate about free will and the right of women to self-determination, even in the matter of mystical visions, when we turned a corner and there, a little further up the hill, was my house. The pale late afternoon sunshine caught the wet slates of the roof and touched them with gold. It looked welcoming and familiar and lovely. Just by the gate were the children standing together, obviously agitated. And suddenly my youngest son turned round and saw me and started actually bouncing with excitement.

'It's Mummy, it's Mummy. Hurrah.'

He scampered down the hill, shedding his anorak as he ran, and hurled himself into my arms. 'We thought you were lost, we thought you'd run away,' he said. His fingers were sticky with jam from somewhere, but he was so pleased to see me that I couldn't complain.

I looked up from his wild embrace and saw the others all surging down the hill after him. For some odd reason they had all thought I was lost; and they were all delighted to see me. It was very gratifying really. They all got a bit over-excited in the end. You know how sometimes release from tension can make you cross, but some other times for no particular reason it can lead to a kind of wild and flamboyant playfulness. This turned into one of those other times and we all got the giggles. And my daughter who is at that excessively maternal age was concerned over my poor blister and demanded that her oldest brother carry me home. Teasing, he swung me up into his arms, although he wasn't quite strong enough to make it feel safe.

'Put me down, you ass,' I said, 'put me down and behave yourselves.'

And for some peculiar reason I heard Angel giggle in a very childish manner. I think what she actually said was 'Rebuke them not, for if these were silent the very stones would cry out', but that doesn't make a lot of sense.

He wouldn't put me down anyway. He carried me into our home and everyone was being very silly, until finally someone managed to upset a large vase of flowers all over the floor. Then we calmed down, and cleared up, but they had got bought crumpets and doughnuts for tea and it was all ready waiting for me like a birthday party. And the good mood and sense of welcome went on all evening and we played Racing Demon and no one fought with anyone.

Sometime during all the carry-on Angel had disappeared, but to be quite honest I really didn't notice. She turned up again at bedtime. I don't know what she thinks I'm likely to get up to just then, but she quite often appears. Secretly I rather enjoy it — being tucked up and kissed good-night. Anyway I was snuggling down and just about ready to put the light out when there she was.

'Did you enjoy it?' she said.

'It was a lovely evening,' I said. And then, so she wouldn't get too carried away with dreams of my becoming a nice suburban middle-aged boring mother, I added dryly 'But what about my mystical vision?' It doesn't do to let your angel get above herself.

She sighed, 'It's absolutely typical. Albeit unearned, I give you a full biblical experience, a triumphal entry into your own city, donkey included *gratis*. And here I am being unselfish and sweet and hard-working and even quite clever getting in all the biblical details, like the house shining like the temple in Jerusalem and substitute palm branches at your feet, and do you congratulate me, or even notice? No, you do not.'

I felt a bit ashamed, but I still wasn't satisfied.

'I'm not satisfied,' I said.

She handed me a book. And illuminated a page of it.

The angels keep their ancient places —
Turn but a stone and start a wing,
'Tis ye, 'tis your estrangéd faces,
That miss the many splendoured thing.

But (when so sad thou canst not sadder)
Cry — and upon thy so sore loss,
Shall shine the traffic of Jacob's ladder
Pitched between heaven and Charing Cross.

I didn't know whether to laugh or cry. Either would have put her in a position of power, so I said 'Well I don't care much for Victorian sentimental religious verse.'

'Don't be such a snob,' she said, preparing to de-materialize. But she was smiling.

'Peace be with you and sleep tight.'

Just as she finally retired she gave me a tiny mystical vision. There were a whole lot of angels going up and down this beautiful ladder, they all looked very like her and they were all smiling; they were also all eating doughnuts, and there was jam on their faces.

I would have thanked her. I really would, only unfortunately I fell asleep.

PEACING IT TOGETHER

&⁊⁊&

I'm not quite sure why I'm telling you this story as a matter of fact. I don't really know what the point of it is. In fact it's a bit silly. But then quite a lot of things are really. Sometimes they're worth telling and sometimes not. Anyway, it's about something that happened to me the other day in my sitting room, about half way between lunch and when the children get home from school.

I was sitting there reading quietly when I heard the all-too-familiar tones of my guardian angel: 'What in God's name is *that*?'

I suppressed a sigh of irritation. I don't know if I've ever told you about my problems with my guardian angel. The thing is that while most people seem to have completely unobtrusive spiritual guides who keep themselves to themselves and even try to disguise their presence, depending entirely on more oblique management techniques (astrology, or evolution, or dialectical materialism, or what have you) mine, presumably because she is too thick for such subtleties, prefers the direct assault. She's always butting in and interrupting my fine thoughts. What's more, while I'm not unique in having an interfering angel, I am — so far as I know — unique in having one who is almost unbelievably stupid. She is also rather dumpy and extremely plain, though now I am a feminist with a raised consciousness I try not to comment on this too much. What's more, she is dead boring: I mean not like Joan's who presented her with mystical voices and led her off to battle and encouraged her to wear drag and command nations and fixed her up with a white horse and a banner and a romantic, if rather painful, death. Most people that I've talked to seem to have heavenly guardian angels, who are radiantly beautiful, spiritually profound, intellectually stimulating and even a bit sexy. Quite frankly, mine is the sort

who, if she were material, would have halitosis and wear exercise
sandals, or something equally grotty. Once in a moment of some
anger I asked her if she were God's punishment on me for being
an uppity feminist, but of course she completely failed to grasp
my heavy irony (have you noticed how *literal* angels are?) and
said with her usual tedious but supernatural patience 'Oh, no,
no no. God doesn't mind *that* at all; what really puts her out is
that whenever you buy doughnuts for the children, you always
get the ones with loose sugar instead of the glazed kind they really
like best.' As I hadn't even noticed that the kids preferred glazed
doughnuts, and also realized in a twinkling that I should have
noticed; and that, moreover, it is only me who really likes the
sugary ones and I don't even eat them — being on an ideologically
unsound diet — I was rather peeved. I mean it is much more fun
to have a God who disapproves of your progressive politics than
a God who prods you about your petty, and in this case purely
imaginative, gluttony.

Anyway, to get back to the point, if there is one: that is the
sort of guardian angel I've got and I do think it's unfair. So you
shouldn't be surprised that I felt some considerable annoyance
when she barged in on my quiet moment, saying, in her slightly
nasal voice, 'What in God's name is *that*?'

'I'm reading,' I said discouragingly.

'I know,' she said, 'but I didn't ask what you were doing,
I asked what that was.' One of her rays illuminated the picture
on my page.

'Nothing much,' I muttered embarrassed; 'I mean nothing
that would interest you. Nothing spiritual.'

'Tut-tut,' she said. 'You never seem to realize how much we
like the material. Much more than you lot like the spiritual, you
know. What is it?'

I knew it would be difficult to explain. The fact is I was
studying this catalogue and trying to decide if I could afford
a tiny — I mean really small — a little bitty nuclear bomb. I
wasn't going to use it or anything. I mean I'm not the aggressive
person around here. I just thought it might be useful to have
around, just in case. But I knew she wouldn't like it. She's really
wet.

'It's a bomb,' I said a bit sullenly.

'A what?' she asked.

'Well, like a firework; it goes off with a big bang and makes a cloud of smoke and a bit of a stink.'

'Hmm,' she said thoughtfully, 'sounds a bit like someone I know. What's it for?'

'Nothing much. It's a sort of status symbol. I suppose you could use it to make bad people behave themselves and things like that. If they were dangerous.'

'You mean *kill them?*' she sounded amazed. And then she made a distinctly snuffly sort of sound. *I'm* amazed for that matter that heaven doesn't fix sinusitis, but lets all these adenoidal angels rush around making a nuisance of themselves. Sometimes I really do wonder if God has got a clue.

'Look,' I said exasperated, 'I'm not planning to use it or anything, but you're always telling me that I don't think about the kids enough and I just thought it would be safer for them if we had one about the house, you know.'

Silence.

'Only in self-defence of course. If everyone was decent I wouldn't want one. But as it is, well I mean, if people knew I had one they wouldn't attack me, would they? Or the kids of course.'

Silence.

'It's no different from judo classes, is it?' She's always trying to get me to stop smoking and take more exercise and one of her more recent so-called brilliant schemes is that I should go to some women's self-defence class and learn judo. So I thought I'd got her there.

'Women enjoy judo classes,' she said.

'So?'

'So that's the difference. Judo is fun; owning a pet bomb and boasting about it to the neighbours isn't. Or shouldn't be.'

I told you she was stupid.

There was a long pause. I tried to pretend she had gone away, but she hadn't. She was hovering somewhere behind my left cortex and looking pained. I just knew she was.

'Sometimes,' I said firmly, and with quite a lot of patience loaded into my expression, 'lacking the supernatural advantages that you lot are lucky enough to possess, you just have to play on their terms. If you're weak they won't respect you, they might even hurt you and they certainly won't listen to you. You need influence. Even Simone Weil said that you had to have prestige, as much or more prestige as they did.' Simone Weil, as I well knew, had not meant exactly that at all, but I felt I could count on Angel not knowing this fact.

Silence.

Not the sort of silence that meant she was thinking about it; the sort of silence that meant she was expecting me to think about it. Suddenly I had this brilliant idea — fighting fire with fire it's called. 'Even you lot go in for it sometimes. What about when you threw the forces of Satan out, huh? War in heaven? Apocalypse now, eh? You can't be passive or pacifistic in the face of evil, can you?'

There was another pause. I thought she was in retreat. I pressed my advantage.

'Come on,' I crowed, 'don't duck. If heaven is allowed wars, why aren't we?'

'I don't know if I should tell you this,' she said quietly, 'God knows what use you'll make of it, but actually we used trampolines.'

'TRAMPOLINES!' I yelled.

'Sure. Trampolines. They really are defensive. You can have one of them if you like. They're fun, like judo.'

I was outraged. And incredulous.

'Look,' she said, 'it's very simple. You set up a line of trampolines and if people want to charge around, they just bounce off. They bounced a long way I admit, poor snakes, but that was mostly our fault because we didn't really understand about gravity. It was before the creation. I expect She was still experimenting. They know they can come back any time they want to play. They're just sulking, that's all. We laughed so much.'

Trampolines. I ask you. But at Christmastime in the trenches of the First World War, both sides played football together; then they hopped back into their trenches and charged each other. A few trampolines might have been a neat idea.

But I was still rather taken with the idea of having my own bomb. Hardly anyone else had got one after all. And this one was a real bargain, relatively speaking. I realized that if I let her know I was impressed by the trampolines, she'd take an unfair advantage. I had to fight on now to defend myself for having started. I tried a new line of attack:

'Trampolines! I don't believe a word of it. And anyway, what about St George?'

'Good heavens,' she exclaimed, 'I thought you of all people ought to know that all that was just an early mediaeval co-option of a variety of pagan stories; typical mythopoeic structure.'

I ask you! It simply is not fair. The last thing you anticipate from angels is de-mystification. Especially when they're stupid.

Well to be quite honest I was so put out and annoyed that I did something I usually discipline myself not to do. I'm not quite sure why it is so with angels, but they don't really like talking about the humanity of Jesus. They seem to like it even less than we like talking about his divinity. If they weren't angels you might think it was because they were envious of us, jealous even. But anyway they do have a way, or at least my angel does, of getting sort of stuffy and distant when you try to discuss it. And she knows she's meant to and she does try hard. So by and large I try to oblige, because after all it isn't really Angel's fault that she is stupid. I always think this kindly tolerance reflects rather well on me. But anyway this time I was so miffed with her pulling that modernist number about St George that I felt she deserved all she got, so I intervened quickly, 'OK then, I'll grant you St George, but what about the temple business. You can't slip out of that one.' I nearly said 'So there!' like a child, but caught myself just in time.

'Temple business?' she likes to pretend innocence sometimes but I am not deceived.

'Temple business,' I said firmly, 'and no, I am not talking about Samson and his pillars. I'm talking about your boss and his aggressive attack on the poor old money lenders doing their job, hurling tables about and bringing not peace but a sword.'

'*Our* boss,' she said, sort of shy but clear.

'OK, then, *our* boss; but you aren't going to dodge this one with word games. Jesus, the incarnate word, God made flesh, like unto us in all matters but sin, gets up on his high horse and starts chucking tables around in a manner which is hardly what we expect from the Prince of Peace. And which certainly does not come into the category of turning the other cheek, loving your enemies, or forgiving those that persecute you.'

I had a moment of pure triumph, I could almost afford to be generous to the vanquished; almost. 'Come on,' I cried, 'a gratuitous act of militancy. What about that then?' Oh I was pleased with myself and my crushing victory. Game, set and match to me I thought with relish.

'Well,' she said, 'I don't know what that has to do with you buying a bomb.'

'Don't you indeed?' I said icily. I was not going to be forced onto the defensive when I had such a good target lined up. 'Well let me explain. We are talking here of the justification for the use of violence against wicked people or their acts. If he is allowed to do that I think I have a good case for my little defensive bomb, don't you.'

'No I don't,' she said, plonkingly. 'In the first place he was angry.'

'So? You get cross when I get angry.'

'Rubbish. I get angry when you misdirect your anger, there's nothing wrong with anger. Anyway don't interrupt. You brought this up not me. In the first place he was angry and with good cause. You know how cross you get when the children make a mess in the house — and anyway it happens also to be their house which was not the case with the temple. In the second place no one was hurt; in the third place it was symbolic, like street theatre. And in the fourth place it was hilarious.'

'Hilarious?' I queried. 'That hardly seems relevant to me.'

'No? Well it wouldn't, would it? You're so selfish. What about us. Here we all were after weeks of being so worried about him, and suddenly he lays on this great show; all those coins flying about, all those panicked market traders looking so shocked and ducking and scrabbling, all that priestly gang shaken out of their pompous self-righteousness and the pigeons flapping in their faces and all his boys laughing so much. And we were all hanging over the edge of heaven in stitches and Gabriel and Michael organizing us in squadrons to go and play too. We hadn't had so much fun in aeons. He was so sweet, the darling, laying that on for our amusement. Tickling us, when really he was in such trouble.'

'Sweet!' I said rather put out. 'Tickling!' I had always rather liked this scene from the Bible, the wrath of God in action, and here she was making it sound like one of the lower moments in a Christmas pantomime. And she never spoke to me in that tender tone.

'Yes,' she said, 'tickling. You wouldn't understand. Oh I get so fed up with you; you're so boring and stupid I sometimes wonder if you're God's punishment on *me* for being such a chatterbox.'

'Well,' I said, still crossly, 'why didn't you come and join in. A can-can chorus line of giggly angels sounds like just what the whole tacky scene needed.'

'That's what we thought too,' she said. There was a pause. 'But he wouldn't let us. He only wanted you lot to play with him and practically none of you would. We would have played and tickled and had fun and we would have looked after him as well. But he didn't want us; he only wanted you. So much that he . . . .'

She stopped. I haven't ever heard her sound like that. She sounded heart broken.

'Look,' I said suddenly, almost surprising myself, 'I won't buy the bloody bomb; I never wanted it anyway.' She wasn't very grateful, considering I was making this sacrifice just to cheer her up.

'I should think not indeed,' she said, like a prissy nanny.

She began to dissolve, sinking faintly into my lower left cranial cavity as usual, preparatory to flowing away into my spinal fluid. 'Peace be with you' she said as she always did prior to departure, trite to the end.

And then she tickled me. Having your brain tickled is ecstatic. It's not a mystical experience actually, it's more sort of, well, fun. I just caught a fading glance of her cheerful grin and peaceable nose and, do you know, just for that moment it did seem to me that she was spiritually profound, radiantly beautiful and even a little bit sexy.

LEGAL PROCEDURES

ᘓᘐᘓ

I'm not sure if this will work out as a story. I'm rather old-fashioned when it comes to stories: I really like a strong plot line and exotic locations, heightened emotions and heightened prose. Even a neat twist at the end. This story has none of the above. In fact it is rather domestic and mundane, though that is entirely the fault of my guardian angel, as you will see. But everyone is into slice-of-life fiction and social realism these days so I thought I might as well give it a go.

My guardian angel put in an appearance the other day, while I was polishing the silver. I sort of hoped she would be impressed to see me performing this menial and housewifely task with such devotion. Of course she wasn't. There's no pleasing her. Not only is she always interrupting me as I go about my humble domestic duties, but she is also always interrupting me when I don't.

I'm beginning to feel that there ought to be a contract or something that you sign, laying down the basic terms of the relationship and renegotiable every couple of years. I can tell you that I'd make my views known at any review: I can just about cope with her having a metaphysical snub nose and wearing a Crimplene angel suit (although you would have thought heaven could run to silk) but I don't see why I should have to put up with this continual nag-nag-nag.

'Hello,' she said in her usual cheery Girl Guide manner.

'Jolly hockey sticks to you too,' I muttered. I thought it was rather a witty riposte, but I was also quite glad she didn't hear it. The last thing I needed that morning was a lecture on the benefits of healthy exercise or a talking-to about my prejudices. Of course I'm not really prejudiced against Girl Guides, it's just a metaphor, a way of talking; but the last time I engaged with Angel along these lines I ended up in a terrible tangle about fascists and 'niggers in woodpiles', 'tarts with hearts' and even the gender of God. So I was perfectly happy to let it go.

'Hmm' she said, in a despicably suspicious voice. 'Well, well, what's all this about?' I tried to tell myself she was peering at my silver with admiration and respect. I was not successful. However I was determined not to surrender.

'I'm polishing the silver,' I said, virtuously. I should say that I am not the sort of person who polishes silver very often, in fact hardly ever. My grandmother left me a small canteen of heavy Victorian cutlery, which usually lives at the back of the cupboard under the stairs; and indeed when I decided this morning that it was entirely imperative that it should be cleaned I had some difficulty in locating it.

'I can see that,' said Angel, 'I'm not stupid.' She is as a matter of fact and I was tempted to say so, but perhaps it wasn't quite the best moment. 'What I'm wondering is why you have chosen this particular morning to polish the silver all of a sudden.'

'It was dirty,' I said.

'It was dirty when you last used it, to try and impress those rather superficial people you had to dinner last April. I pointed it out to you then, and you didn't clean it.'

'They weren't superficial,' I said indignantly, 'she was famous.' I realized that I would much rather argue with Angel about those dinner guests, even though they were superficial and I had only invited them because I got a buzz out of telling my friends, than I would pursue the question about why I was polishing the silver.

But Angel couldn't be diverted. 'We are meant to be talking about why you were polishing the silver,' she said. I bet they send trainee guardian angels to assertiveness classes; they always insist on talking about what they want. It's very selfish.

'I would have thought you would have approved of my performing so womanly a task,' I said irritably.

'Dear God, you are stupid,' she exclaimed. 'It cannot — surely it cannot — have escaped even your notice that you only perform these "womanly tasks" as you call them on those occasions when you have something serious on your conscience.'

My stomach lurched. Not only was it true, but it had indeed escaped my notice. I didn't only feel bad, I also felt foolish. It was extremely irritating; the last thing anyone needs from her guardian angel is being made to feel foolish.

'Go dance on the head of a pin,' I said rudely. It was childish, but better than nothing.

'No more space,' she said calmly, 'the answer isn't infinity.' I bit my lip before asking what the answer was. I suspected she was smiling at her own cleverness and I was not going to indulge her.

'Well,' she said, after a pause, 'what is going on here?'

'Don't nag me,' I said.

'We have a definition of nagging in heaven,' she said, with every appearance of serene helpfulness; 'you might find it useful, especially now you're a feminist. "Nagging is someone asking you a second time for something you ought to have given them the first time and you still don't want to." ' There was a pause, during which I was rather impressed by this definition. Then she said, with a faint hint of weariness, 'Well, and this is for the third time of asking, what is going on here?'

'You tell me, if you're such a know-it-all.'

'I did sort of wonder if it had anything at all to do with this morning's visit by that curiously sulphur-scented gentleman, the chairman of your Residents' Support Group,' she said.

Angels have a very peculiar sense of smell. Mine does anyway; she's always complaining about odours of singeing and sulphur and so on; and I for one have never noticed anything remotely ill-perfumed about Allan Smotherington, who is the chair of our local residents' group, and had indeed paid me a visit that very morning. However, just then I was more interested in Angel's admission than in the sensitivity of angelic nostrils.

'So you were there!' I had been suspicious at the time. I had thought I could feel the odd twanging of synapses in my frontal lobes, which is one of the many irritating ways in which Angel makes her presence known to me, but they had been very faint and I had ignored them. 'That is totally despicable,' I shouted, 'sneaking around like a thief in the night, spying, lurking, under-hand, dishonest, covert . . . .'

'Oh shut up,' said Angel, sharply for her. 'Did you sign his petition?'

I hesitated. The thing was that Allan, after being extremely agreeable and commenting on my children's beautiful manners

and on my roses' beautiful condition, had asked me to sign a
petition. Someone had applied for planning permission to turn
the small hotel at the top of the street into a hostel for people
with AIDS, and Allan did not think that the premises were terribly suitable for that sort of use. He knew an awful lot about
it too, about fire precautions and whether the hill was too steep
for people who were already weak and so on. It probably wasn't
at all suitable really.

'You did sign it, didn't you?' Angel said. She sounded appalled,
though not half as appalled as I was that heaven permitted angels
to go about practically using third degree on their suspects.

I didn't say anything. She knew as well as I did that I had
signed his petition. 'I'm not surprised under the circumstances',
she said coldly, 'that a certain amount of tarnish removal seemed
like a sensible idea this morning.'

There was a pause.

'For the love of God, why?' I didn't answer, as I was in the
middle of rubbing very hard at an obstinate black mark on the
handle of a fork.

'I'm beginning to feel', she went on, 'that there ought to
be a contract or something that you sign, laying down the basic
terms of the relationship and renegotiable every couple of years.
And I can tell you that I would be very clear at any review: I
can just about cope with you being a metaphysical moron and
expecting angels to wear silk (although you would have thought
feminism might have done something about that) but I don't see
why I should have to put up with this continual petty desire
to be thought well of. Even by snakes in the grass like Allan
Smotherington.'

She wrinkled up her nose and sniffed disdainfully; even I
could catch a distant whiff of sizzling flesh. It was true that
men like Allan always intimidated me. I wondered desperately if
Angel was going to submit a written report on me; I wondered if
she already had; I wondered if God had a moustache like Allan's
— which was silky when pleased and bristly when not. It was
pretty scary. I tried to explain.

'It wasn't because I was scared of him. It wasn't that. It
was a compromise, an arrangement.'

'Flower arrangements, yes; moral arrangements, no,' said
Angel; it sounded like a particularly inane political slogan.

'It's all right for you,' I said, 'you're an anarchic Trotskyite. And a puritan.'

'I am not,' she said firmly, 'I'm an angel.'

'Same difference. You simply don't live in the real world.'

'True,' she said, and said it with an infuriating air of complacency.

'Look,' I said, 'I know it wasn't right in itself, and I didn't want to sign, but we made a deal. He's going to withdraw his opposition to the playground extension.' I thought that Angel would be pleased; she's been working with me for nearly two years to get the playground extended; the kids round here, including my youngest son, really need it. But Angel looked entirely bored.

'More than that,' I said, 'he's going to support it at the next council meeting, and he's going to talk to the councillor in the next-door ward and they are going to arrange . . .' I went on and on with elaborate details of how Allan Smotherington had spun a delightful little web of contacts and connections and how they would all fit together and the only thing needed to make it all work was that I should sign a silly petition opposing the unnecessary use of a highly unsuitable site. And I explained it to her in detail so that she would understand that it was just a little tiny compromise. Although really I knew that Allan Smotherington had not been telling the truth — or rather he hadn't been telling the real truth about why he didn't want the hostel.

Throughout all this Angel paid absolutely no attention. Instead she started fiddling with the silver. About when I got to the council meeting she picked up a couple of spoons, and then a fork or two and began to juggle with them. She added a ladle, and then half a dozen knives. They spun, glittering and sparkling in the air, like a waterfall of silver.

I had reached the crucial point about dealing with the poll-tax budget shortfall and how it might well be the turning-point for the next election, when she deftly added the rest of the dessert spoons and three cake forks. I forgot to be annoyed. I was stunned and delighted. It was so seldom she would show off her angelic powers for me. She reached out for an additional handful of teaspoons.

'Angel,' I murmured, awed, 'that's beautiful!' I was glad I had cleaned them; flowing through her hands was a river, a fountain of silver. 'How many pieces can you do?' I said greedily.

'Thirty. Thirty pieces of silver.'

And she let them all crash to the ground, like tinkling brass and clanging cymbals.

'Angel,' I cried, 'don't do that!' But she dematerialized so abruptly that I was left with a sharp ache in my lumbar region.

The kitchen was a mess. It was all very well for her to sneer at what she called 'womanly tasks', but I now had a kitchen floor covered with spoons and forks, a spilled tin of silver polish, which really does smell hellish, and an incredibly busy day ahead of me. I really wanted to complain to the higher management, but felt I wasn't in a strong negotiating position.

She didn't turn up again until late in the afternoon. I was in the garden, and when she commented on the beautiful condition of my roses I realized just how insincere Allan Smotherington had been that morning. She seemed a bit shy and, for her, quiet.

Finally she said 'I'm sorry. I was showing off.'

'You were right,' I said, and even saying it made me feel grouchy again, because I still can't work out how anyone so stupid can be right so often.

'Gin and tonic?' she offered hesitantly. I accepted gratefully because angelic g. and t.s are not things to be turned down. We sipped them together beside the rose bushes.

'Well,' she said, 'you must be feeling exhausted, but I would like to point out that if you hadn't been so stupid in the first place you wouldn't have had to rush round all day.'

'True,' I said tiredly. It had been hard work. I had had to remove my name from Allan's petition, endure his hysterical-women-who-don't-know-their-own-minds rant, find a shop that would buy the silver, send a cheque to the AIDS charity *and* set up the beginnings of a little political web of my own including a petition in support of having a playground in the garden of the proposed hostel.

'But', I said, trying for exactly her own smug tone, 'if I hadn't been so stupid I wouldn't be enjoying this heavenly drink.'

She looked put upon, as she often does. 'Really, you know it doesn't work like that. Divine gin and tonics, like justification, are not earned by good works. They are freely given.' She got ready to dissolve, but warmly and softly this time. Just as she was going I said 'Hey, I really liked the juggling.'

'That was nothing,' she said. 'Peace be with you.' And as she sank into the bottom of my skull she performed a quick juggling stunt with seventy stars and thirty-three haloes, all trailing clouds of glory.

AFTER SUPPER

&⟡&

There are a lot of things in life that I don't understand very well, and one of them is how you know before you start whether a story is going to be worth telling. This one is a case in point, or perhaps without point. It's about something that happened to me one Thursday evening, and perhaps it is about the complexity and richness of life, and perhaps it is about nothing at all. You just have to tell it and then see, really, and by that time it's too late.

Another thing I don't understand in life — and I think this does have something to do with this story — is why I am afflicted with a guardian angel as totally uninterested in spirituality and theology as mine is. I mean I'm not a raging intellectual or anything but I'm not totally uneducated and I do have a few abstract interests. So I am constantly amazed that I should have been lumbered with a guardian angel who doesn't seem to have any insight into the finer points of metaphysics. I asked her about this once, but she only said 'Luck of the draw. Or otherwise', in a tone that I did not find endearing.

She doesn't seem to understand that it is very frustrating when I say to her 'I think I am entering into the Dark Night of the Soul' and all she replies is 'Pre-menstrual tension: buy some oil of evening primrose'.

Or I get really interested in Thomas Aquinas's theories about minor heresies, and she giggles and says 'Do you know, he was so fat that they had to carve a semi-circle out of the refectory table so he could eat comfortably?'

And actually I didn't know, and it does make a difference doesn't it, but that isn't the point. You really don't expect to be allocated a guardian angel who chatters on like a gossip columnist, and is only interested in ticking you off for terribly petty little offences and generally making your life a misery and lowering your aspirations.

In my opinion it cannot be the job of angels to keep you down to earth.

Once when Angel was on her sabbatical leave (as you have probably noticed angels are oddly strict about this), I got a fabulous supply-angel. He was devastatingly beautiful for a start, and without wanting to sound too trivial, this does raise the tone of things. He really dressed the part, and would arrive fluttering rose-scented pinions and flowing drapes. This is in marked, and to my mind admirable, contrast to Angel who, poor dear, is not only unfortunately plain but also tends to go more for the non-corporeal version of baggy acrylic jerseys and sensible wool skirts. He was really trendy and encouraged me to go on spiritual pilgrimages (which luckily you can do while still staying comfortably at home) and listen to music instead of saying formulaic boring old prayers, and he was into liturgical dance and praying in tongues and relaxation and astrology. But when Angel came home, all she did was poke around inside my cranium for a bit and then say 'You forgot to send your mother a birthday card.'

Well, it was true as a matter of fact and my mother was really hurt, but I wasn't going to tell Angel that. So I quoted, 'Anyone who will not leave mother and father to follow after me is not worthy of the Gospel.'

I'm sorry to say that the only reward I got for my devout biblicism was a very nasty headache and three days of infantile sulking by Angel.

All this was meant to be an aside, but I have only to think about my guardian angel to get into a foul temper, because there is something totally unjust about it all. No one else seems to have these difficulties. Anyway, you need to understand how miserably inadequate Angel is to make much sense of this story.

Well, as I was saying, one Thursday evening Angel turned up just as we were finishing supper. And without wanting to get diverted again this does seem to me an excellent illustration of the problem: who wants to have spiritual converse with their guardian angel when they are trying to negotiate with three teenagers and a nine-year-old, all of whom are being completely unreasonable and extremely selfish?

Angels, in my opinion, are meant to manifest themselves in quiet and reflective moments — about half way through the second psalm at Cathedral Evensong for example, and during solitary walks on long sunny evenings.

They are not meant to insinuate themselves into your kitchen at the precise moment when, provoked beyond all possible human endurance, you start to scream at your children. If they insist on arriving at times when the precious soul, for whom they are, I presume, responsible to the eternal God is in such serious trouble, then I do expect at least a small lightning bolt, just enough to scare a temperamental thirteen-year-old into a little respect for her mother, or a clap of thunder loud enough to persuade a nine-year-old that he would really like to be in bed.

What they are not meant to do is heave wheezy sighs with faintly martyred undertones, and then with long-suffering smiles begin to do your washing-up. And they are absolutely not meant to hum clearly, though inaudibly, verses from nineteenth-century hymns.

Angel, you will probably not be surprised to hear, did all of the things that angels are not meant to do. The hymn she selected was 'Forty days and forty nights' and she dwelt with loathsome relish on the verse that goes

> So shall we have peace divine;
> Holier gladness ours shall be;
> Round us too shall angels shine,
> Such as ministered to thee.

'Oh shut up,' I yelled.

This was more than my middle son was prepared to put up with. In his usual egocentric way he imagined that I had been addressing him. He flounced from the house, swearing with typical adolescent hysteria, that he had been trying to tell me the most important thing in his life and that it was impossible to have decent conversation with someone who wasn't interested and that I didn't care about him and that I was the most selfish woman in the world. He was leaving home and he was never coming back. The door slammed.

This exhibition was followed by what must be the most frightening of all the sounds in the world, the snarling and growling and roaring of a furious motorbike. Even my daughter, with all the sang-froid of thirteen, was impressed.

Hours later I grunted at Angel 'It wasn't my fault.'

All the response I got was one of her best silences.

I'm not sure if I've ever mentioned this, but Angel is better at silences than anyone. Not just loaded silences, but breeched and aimed as well. Not just pregnant, but in advanced labour. I have repeatedly asked Angel about this skill, rather thinking I might acquire it for myself, as it appears to be the most efficient way of inducing guilt even in the comparatively innocent, but all she does is look a bit shy and say that all celestial beings can do it because of timeless practice before The Throne. I don't find this helpful. I'm not sure I even believe her really because my attempts at adoration have exactly the opposite effect. I suspect her of holding out on me.

Sometime later I said 'It's all my fault.'

The response to this magnanimity was no different. Just more silence. She was there all right, hovering. I can always tell. But she was silent.

Sometime later I said 'It was both our faults.'

She condescended to reply to that. She said 'That's no excuse for refusing to read the little one's story.' I ask you!

'I'm too worried,' I told her crossly.

'So was he,' she said.

I got up and went towards the stairs, up which I had previously exiled my tearful youngest son. Angel said 'And if you wake him up to ease your conscience I really might get cross.'

'I wasn't going to,' I said.

'Oh, good,' she said blandly. Then she went on 'If you really want to engage in a wee sample of guilt-induced amateur theatricals, you could try doing it with your daughter. She'd genuinely enjoy it.'

No one who has met my daughter would *ever* think of competing with her in a full-scale 'how-much-drama-can-I-get-out-of-this-situation' competition. Frankly there would be no contest. My daughter is as good at out-emoting others as Angel is at out-silencing them. I decided to assume that Angel's suggestion was yet another of her schemes for my humiliation.

After another longish silence, I said 'All right then, what should I do?'

'Watch and pray,' said Angel, 'watch and pray, lest you enter into temptation.'

'I'm too angry,' I said. 'You can't pray when you're angry.'

'I can,' said Angel, in what seemed to me to be rather a self-satisfied way.

'Sadly,' I said, with what — under the circumstances — seemed to me to be an impressively ironic voice, 'I am but a poor mortal and not designed in the "continually do pray" mode.'

'I thought you disliked the use of Victorian hymns?'

'I think I'll try praying,' I said quickly. That was one activity she never interrupted.

I did try. When the telephone went I had only just dropped off to sleep. Actually I wasn't really asleep, just dozing.

'I wasn't asleep,' I told Angel. 'I was praying. In fact I may have been in a trance.'

'I doubt it,' said Angel. 'Although it is not entirely without precedent, I can assure you that it is very unusual to snore when in any advanced spiritual condition, except of course sleep. Perhaps you had better answer the telephone.'

I did. He was fine. He was sorry. He sounded tearful and distraught. He really had wanted to tell me something terribly important.

'What?' I asked him, but he couldn't tell me on the phone. Could he come home now? Would I wait up for him, please?

Of course I would.

I asked Angel what he wanted to tell me, but she wouldn't say.

'But I need to know. So I can pray better . . .' You'd think that any self-respecting, professionally competent Angel would be thrilled to co-operate with so pious and maternal a desire. She really can be a complete drag.

'Whatever can it be?'

'God knows,' she said.

Then it dawned on me that perhaps she didn't know and was covering up her ignorance. So I started on what I hoped would be a crafty investigation as to the level of prevenient knowledge permitted to angels; I thought I might trap her into boasting, but it didn't work. After a while she said 'I really don't like talking shop. It's extremely late. Why don't you just pray.'

So I did. And when I woke up it was past midnight.

Angel was still there. She said, quite tenderly for her, 'It's all right, you can sleep now.'

My son had pinned a large notice to the wall in front of me. It said 'Everything's OK now. I love you. Sleep well.'

'Angel,' I said. 'What happened?'

'He came in. You were asleep. I think he was disappointed at first; he seemed lonely and tired. He sort of tried to wake you, but you snuggled down and started snoring. So then he grinned and wrote the note and went to bed.'

'But what did he want to tell me? What was going on?'

'That is something that you will never know, something you would have known if you'd been paying attention when he asked you to. Bad luck.'

'Angel!'

'It's not my secret, I can't tell you.'

'But he's my son!'

And then she looked at me, and said 'Anyone who will not leave mother and father to follow after me is not worthy of the Gospel. Who is my mother, who are my brothers and sisters? Those who hear the word of God and keep it.'

The nerve of it. I told you she was impossible. I tried once more.

'I think you have a moral responsibility to tell me,' I said.

'You are the one who likes theology so much,' she said, a little bitchily I thought, 'so I will tell you something. God has no grandchildren. Only children.'

And with that she prepared to depart. I was tired and cold and cross and worried. I had failed to meet my son's needs and I had made a fool of myself. But as I felt her warm and fluid passage into my spinal column, I also felt an enormous sense of relief. Because I wasn't solely responsible for the children, or because someone would treat me like a child. I was too tired to work out which.

'Peace be with you,' I said to Angel, at exactly the same moment as she said it to me. I had never managed that before.

At the last possible instant she said 'As well as being very fat and very absent-minded, Thomas Aquinas snored very, very loudly.'

BAD FRIDAY

&⁀&

I have a bit of a problem with this story. It's not really like some of the other stories about my somewhat tiresome guardian angel.

For one thing it happened in the night.

Oddly enough — well it does seem odd to me — my guardian angel does not often appear in the night. As a matter of fact, I strongly suspect that this is because she has such a pathetic imagination. She can't cope with dreams, and is confined to the daily. You read in the Bible of truly wonderful dreams; like Jacob's ladder or Joseph putting his brothers in their place by boasting about their measly little sheaves of corn bowing down to his great big fat one.

I think a few dreams would be fun, and a much better way of getting spiritual guidance because you could chat for hours with your friends about interpretations and Freud and sex and things. But do I dream? No, I don't. All I get are her clichés, and her interfering pettiness, and her tedious scruples.

Of course, she doesn't agree. She says the reason I don't get dreams is because I sleep so soundly, for which — in her opinion — I ought to be grateful. I find this terribly unromantic, but it's true: frankly the minute I turn the light out I slump asleep and practically never wake up again until the alarm clock rings. But you might well think a half-way competent angel would be able to deal with such a minor impediment. It makes you wonder. If I were God the very least I'd do is check that all the guardian angels had *some* creative flair, and ones like mine who are so totally prosaic and mundane would be kept in heaven, well out of the way of delicate and aspiring souls.

Anyway, all this is pretty irrelevant because as it happens this story did take place in the night. At twelve minutes past three to be precise. The very worst imaginable time to be woken up by an angel with a slightly common accent manifesting herself all of a sudden, and saying 'I've just popped in to say goodbye.'

'Go away,' I muttered. In my own defence I must stress that I was nine-tenths asleep. Then I remembered with a horrid jerk that I had said much the same thing to my daughter one night when she was ten years old and had been woken up two hours later by my very angry oldest son reporting that she was retching and shivering and swallowing her pain in the bathroom, and telling him not to wake me or I would be cross. She had acute appendicitis; and had been wheeled into surgery still apologizing for having disturbed me.

(By the way, in fairness since I am always complaining about Angel, I should mention that she was completely marvellous that night, and came with us all the way in the ambulance and did try to comfort me, and reassure me that I could go on being a mother. Unlike usual, she didn't rub my face in guilt. I refused her consolation though — I knew all about my inadequacy and awfulness on that occasion.)

So with that unfortunate precedent looming in my consciousness I sat up and said 'Sorry, Angel, I was asleep. Is it something important?'

'I just popped in to say goodbye.'

'Can't that wait?' I asked peevishly.

'You are always telling me you want divine revelations in the cold small hours of the night,' she said. If anyone else had used that tone to me I would have thought they were being a bit sarcastic, but Angel is too dense for such subtleties.

'I don't see your departure exactly as a spiritual revelation,' I muttered. And then it hit me. Her departure. She couldn't leave me, not just like that. I hadn't been *that* nasty to her; it was just that we disagreed about quite a lot of things. Surely angels could accept and tolerate difference? Surely she wouldn't be that small-minded? What did she expect, slavish obedience or something? Not that I minded of course; if she wanted to desert her God-given duties that was up to her; it was none of my business. It was just the principle of the thing.

'Angel . . .' I began.

'You know we always take this Friday off,' she said.

She always did too. Regular as clockwork. 'Fine,' I said, ignoring a great surge of relief and happiness, 'I don't see why you had to wake me up for that. Did you think I'd forget or something? See you Easter Day.'

There was a pause. Then she said, with what sounded like an unusual degree of diffidence, 'I thought I'd better remind you about fasting.'

'Fasting! For Good Friday!' I exclaimed. 'Oh don't be so antiquated. No one does that anymore.'

She didn't argue with me, there was just one of her long silences.

'I'm not', I said boldly, 'into all that body-hating, masochistic, mediaeval stuff. Do you fast in heaven?'

Her silence continued. I waited hopefully. For once, I thought, I had her where I wanted her. In the wrong. After a bit I heard her sniffle; the poor thing was probably embarrassed. I felt a moment of compassion, but, thinking about all the times she had forced me to apologize, I clung to my moment of triumph.

'Well,' I said, after I thought she had been silent for long enough, 'do you fast in heaven?'

The silence went on a bit longer. It was almost beginning to feel awkward; then she said, quite suddenly and almost crossly for her, 'Well we can't, can we? We don't eat. We don't feel hunger.'

But the odd thing was that she didn't sound the least bit pleased with herself — either for her minor victory over me, or for this abundant proof of the superiority of angels.

We fell into silence again. It went on for a long time. I thought she had finished harassing me and would dematerialize herself in her own good time, so I lay down again and tried to go back to sleep. She was still there, hovering in my left cortex as only angels can. Now and again she made a funny snuffly sound, as though she had a cold; but when someone has just reminded you, and in rather a disagreeable tone, that they don't experience hunger, you can't very well offer them a handkerchief and tell them to blow their nose.

It was all very annoying. I felt more and more obstinate. She could stay or go in her own good time, but I was not going to initiate another conversation. It was three o'clock in the morning, for goodness sake, and no time for a busy woman to be having to deal with sulky angels. And in passing I would like to say that no human being, not even the adolescent male, can sulk as efficiently and thoroughly as your average angel. All I wanted was to go back to sleep.

The snuffling however did not diminish. On the contrary. Then I realized that she was crying. I mean really crying. It was a bit embarrassing actually, like the first time a grown-up man cries those terrible awkward male tears onto you; you know it's a sort of compliment, you have an inkling of how much they need to do it, and, at the same time, you just wish they wouldn't, because they are so bad at it. Angel's tears made me squirm a bit; I nearly asked her how it was that angels could cry when they couldn't eat, and then decided that would not be very kind. But I really did feel quite strongly that it was an angel's rôle to comfort not to be comforted, so I let her get on with it for a bit.

In the end it got to me; that irrepressible maternal instinct — or since I'm a feminist perhaps I should say human instinct — that simply prevents you from letting a person, or I suppose an angel for that matter, cry. I wasn't best pleased about it.

'Oh for heaven's sake, Angel,' I said, when I could bear it no longer, 'whatever's the matter now?'

But she didn't reply. She just went on crying. It was really getting on my nerves. I said 'All right then, if it means that much to you I will fast today.'

You might think that this generosity of spirit would cheer anyone up, but it didn't work with her.

'Please.' I could hear myself begging. When I think of all the times that she has felt free to interrupt me and demand that I talk to her about whatever idiotic banality she chooses. And now she was refusing me the same privilege. It wasn't fair. That sounded a bit childish, so I changed my mind. It was outrageous!

'You're behaving like a teenager,' I said; I tried to say it firmly rather than angrily. Three teenage children in one household is quite enough, without having to put up with a teenaged spiritual force that skulked about somewhere slightly above my top vertebra. Once my daughter locked herself in the bathroom and howled for three hours, and when she finally came out she demanded cinnamon toast and refused point blank ever to say what the matter was. I was not going through that again, especially not with a blasted angel about whom I could not even have the dubious satisfaction of murmuring 'boy-friend-trouble' with the world-weariness of middle age.

'Angel,' I said, 'don't be such a baby.' But when babies cry you can comfort them. You can kiss them and cuddle them; you can wrap them warm and safe against you, petting their pink, flushed faces. You can find their favourite teddy bear, its face already worn bald with the receiving of love and the giving of furry comfort. You cannot do any of these things, or anything like them, with an angel. Grey matter may be soft and warm, but cuddly it is not. I reached through my mind and spirit for tenderness and comfort and found my hands empty. It was very frustrating.

The crying went on and on. I had tried emotional bribery and I had tried emotional blackmail. There was nothing left except love. And, given the difficulties of our relationship, and the degree to which I felt irritated by her, it was not an easy thing to offer.

'Angel,' I said, as carefully as I knew how. 'I love you. When you came to say goodbye I had forgotten about the Friday bank holiday or whatever you call it in heaven, and I thought you were leaving me permanently. I was sad. I didn't even know I was sad, but I was. I was sad because I love you. And because I need you. But honestly I would rather you left me if that made you happier than have you stay like this.'

I felt a complete idiot when I said this. There are many things you find yourself doing as you get older which your optimistic young self would never have known how to dream of, but very high on that list for me comes sitting up in bed at four in the morning, in a flannel nightie, trying to tell *anyone*, let alone a weeping and unresponsive citizen of heaven, that you love her.

But it worked. Not magically or instantaneously or anything, but the solid flow of desolate tears turned back into the infuriating adenoidal snuffles, and then into the hiccups of a sob-exhausted toddler.

Finally she said 'It's worse than you know.'

'What is?' I asked, relieved that we were getting somewhere, but weary with the strain.

'I'm jealous.'

'Jealous!' I exclaimed startled. 'Jealous?' I inquired in an attempt at non-judgemental open-minded interest.

There was a bit more snuffling, and then finally she said 'I'm jealous of *you*.'

'Me?' I said tentatively, though really I meant 'What on earth are you talking about?'

'Yes you. I'm jealous of you because you can get hungry. Because you can get hurt, I mean physically hurt, because you can have pain, and suffering, and agony.'

'But that's not nice. I mean, those things aren't nice. They're horrid. Why does that make you jealous?'

'Because you can be with Him today and we can't. We just can't. We tried and tried and we couldn't understand. After the Last Supper he went away from us. We thought we could rescue him and he wouldn't let us. Then we thought at least we could comfort him, and we couldn't. That peasant woman could; she may be the Queen of Heaven now, but then she was just a middle-aged woman from the sticks, but she could comfort him, and her half-daft fisherman friend and that red-headed whore from Magdala; they could comfort him because they could understand. And we, the first-born of the creation, the spinners of the seven spheres, the messengers of the Holy Spirit, the powers and dominions, cherubim and seraphim, angels and archangels; we could do nothing. He didn't need us. We could not go where he had gone. We could not understand. That's why we all take the day off; not for a holiday but because we know we're useless.

'They scourged him and we could not feel it. They crowned him with thorns and it didn't hurt us. They banged those nails through his hands and we wept for his humiliation, but we could not go where he had gone when he went into the pain-place, whatever that is. He gave you the glory, the privilege of going where he went, into the body in all its beauty and holiness, into the pain and the pleasure of the flesh. He loves you more than he loves us. And you take that privilege, that gift, that joy so lightly that you don't even care enough to fast once a year. *Of course I'm jealous.*'

She began to cry again. So did I, as a matter of fact. We wept together and we could not comfort each other.

'We don't call it Good Friday,' she gulped after a while, 'we call it Bad Friday.'

'Angel,' I said, 'I really will fast today. I'll fast for me and I'll fast for you.' This time the generosity of spirit was slightly more authentic.

'Thank you,' she said.

It was nearly dawn, grey light was coming through the curtains. She got ready to depart. I began to think about how impressed my children would be when they saw I wasn't eating, not even the hot cross buns. It might even reconvert my middle son who was trying out existentialism at that moment. I might even become a great ascetic saint pretty soon, known for the rigours of my life and for my charity to lesser mortals.

Angel put a stop to that; she paused in her soft descent through my cranial cavity, and murmured 'Watch it, sister; we haven't even started on hair shirts and flagellation yet, and they're tough.' But she was grinning a shy, happy, little grin.

'Peace be with you,' she said as usual, 'and see you on Sunday.'